ENTREPRENEUR SECRETS

Real Stories of Purpose, Profit, and Power

**24 Elite Business Leaders
With Peter Remington**

ENTREPRENEUR SECRETS
Real Stories of Purpose, Profit, and Power

Copyright © 2026 PETER REMINGTON. All rights reserved.

No part of this book may be reproduced in any form or by any mechanical means, including information storage and retrieval systems, without permission in writing from the publisher or author, except by a reviewer who may quote passages in a review. All images, logos, quotes, and trademarks included in this book are subject to use according to trademark and copyright laws of the United States of America.

REMINGTON, PETER, Author
ENTREPRENEUR SECRETS
PETER REMINGTON

Published by:
ELITE ONLINE PUBLISHING
63 East 11400 South
Suite #230
Sandy, UT 84070
EliteOnlinePublishing.com

ISBN: 979-8-9993587-2-1 (Paperback)
ISBN: 979-8-9993587-3-8 (eBook)

BUS071000
BUS046000

QUANTITY PURCHASES: Schools, companies, professional groups, clubs, and other organizations may qualify for special terms when ordering quantities of this title. For information, email Peter@PeterRemington.com.

All rights reserved by PETER REMINGTON.
This book is printed in the United States of America.

ACKNOWLEDGEMENTS

I want to acknowledge every author involved in the creation of this educational, motivational, inspirational, and transparent business book. Having read each chapter numerous times, a common theme emerged: tenacity and the overall belief that each author had in the dream. Even though the path to their success took varying amounts of time, each author stayed focused until they achieved their desired outcome. It reminds me of two simple but powerful statements.

"Everything happens on time. Not necessarily on your time, But on time. God's time."

"Lack of evidence is not evidence of lack."

Meaning all your efforts are not going unnoticed. Unfortunately, there isn't a sonogram to show you how your manifestation is growing, only belief.

Thank you to Jacqui, Bill, Matt, Gerard, Adrian, Lary, Theresa, Helen, Saba, Kimberly, Trace, Steven, Charles, Gretchen, Dawn, Edward, Alicia, Mickey, Romain, Tod, Beth, Joe, Taft, and Karen for their contributions and belief.

Additionally, I want to thank the team of Elite Online Publishing, Melanie, and Jenn for producing the book.

Finally, I want to thank myself. This was one hell of a project!

–Peter Remington

All proceeds from the sale of this book will go to Kids' Meals

A Houston-based charity that feeds over 10,000 preschool children daily.

TABLE OF CONTENTS

Acknowledgements	iii
Foreword	1
Chapter 1 Building a Business, Building a Life: My Journey as a Real Estate Entrepreneur *By Bill Baldwin*	5
Chapter 2 From Barriers to Breakthroughs *By Dr. Jacquie Baly*	13
Chapter 3 Waking Up with Purpose *By Lary Barton*	21
Chapter 4 Building Beyond the Blueprint: How Vision and Strategy Drive Success *By Steven Lawrence Biegel, AIA, LEED AP*	31
Chapter 5 A Crash Course in Resilience: Opening a Restaurant in the Middle of a Pandemic *By Matt Brice, CEO and Founder, Federal American Grill*	41
Chapter 6 Where Purpose Meets the Plate *By Charles Clark*	47
Chapter 7 You. Only Better. *By Kimberly Sherer Cutchall*	55

Chapter 8 The Beginning: From Reluctant Salesperson to Passionate Professional
By Karen DeGeurin 69

Chapter 9 The Design of a Life: My Entrepreneurial Blueprint
By Adrian Dueñas 77

Chapter 10 From Markets to Media: My Journey Through Entrepreneurship, Mentorship, and Chaos
By Tod Eason 85

Chapter 11 A Community Built on Bees
By Gretchen Gilliam 93

Chapter 12 Building More Than Meals: My Journey with Kids' Meals
By Beth Harp 103

Chapter 13 A Love Letter
By Alicia Jansen 111

Chapter 14 From Dreamer to Doer
By Romain Kapadia 121

Chapter 15 From the Gridiron to the Beaches of Normandy— A Journey of Legacy, Purpose, and Remembrance
Joe Machol 131

Chapter 16 A Life Built on Purpose, Not Perfection
By Taft McWhorter 139

Chapter 17 The Imagination Blueprint—From Dream to Enterprise
By Dawn Nelson MSW, CPC 149

Chapter 18 Patron of Persistence
By Gerard A. OBrien 159

Chapter 19 A Life Built on Numbers: Entrepreneurs Turn Vision into Value and Value into Equity
By Mickey O'Neal — 167

Chapter 20 Impression Management
By Helen Sage Perry — 179

Chapter 21 Unapologetic, Unbreakable, Unstoppable
By Theresa Roemer — 191

Chapter 22 The ArchedBeauty™ 4-D Brow Revolution: Redefining the Frame of the Face
By Edward Sanchez — 199

Chapter 23 Dreaming Out Loud
By Trace J. Sherer — 207

Chapter 24 Rising From Within
By Saba Syed — 215

Chapter 25 How to Become a Swinger!
By Peter C. Remington — 223

> **What the mind can conceive and believe,
> a person can achieve.**
>
> *—Napolean Hill*

FOREWORD

The Purpose, Profit, and Power of the Entrepreneurial Spirit

Entrepreneurs are the heartbeat of every thriving economy. They are the risk-takers, the dreamers, the doers' individuals who don't just envision change but act on it. They come from every walk of life. Some launched their ventures straight out of school, driven by a vision too bold to ignore. Others pivoted mid-career, fueled by lessons learned and a desire to chart their own course. Still others waited until retirement or a major life shift to finally pursue the idea that had lived in the back of their mind for decades. Regardless of when they began, one truth remains consistent: entrepreneurs shape the fabric of our cities, communities, and industries in ways that are both visible and deeply felt.

The journey of an entrepreneur is not a straight path. It's rarely glamorous and often riddled with sleepless nights, financial uncertainty, self-doubt, and unexpected detours. But for those who dare to take the leap, it is one of the most rewarding and transformative paths a person can take. Being your own boss means owning the risk and the reward. It means wearing every hat until you can afford to hire help. It means trusting your instincts when the data is incomplete and staying resilient when the market shifts overnight. It means leading with vision, integrity, and grit even when no one is watching.

Entrepreneurs play an indispensable role in the economy. They create jobs, stimulate innovation, and bring vitality to industries both new and old. But beyond economics, entrepreneurs bring something even more valuable: leadership. They rally people around a cause. They build cultures where creativity can thrive. They empower others to think differently, to solve problems in new ways, and to take ownership of their own professional paths. A single entrepreneur can change the trajectory of a neighborhood, revitalize a local economy, or create a ripple effect that inspires the next generation of leaders.

In cities across America and especially in growing, diverse cities, entrepreneurs are not just building businesses; they're building legacies. They're opening restaurants that become cultural institutions. They're launching tech startups that draw global attention. They're creating nonprofits that serve the underserved. They're mentoring the next wave of business owners, speaking in schools, investing in their communities, and showing others what's possible when passion meets purpose.

What's remarkable about the entrepreneurial community is that it is as varied as it is vibrant. There is no single mold for an entrepreneur. Some begin with venture capital; others bootstrap every dollar. Some have MBAs; others have hard-earned street smarts. Some start with a storefront; others start with a laptop at their kitchen table. But all share a common trait: the courage to begin and the tenacity to keep going.

This collection of stories and insights is a gift to you from twenty-four entrepreneurs who dared to believe that they could build something better for themselves, for their families, and for their communities. It honors not just the businesses they've built, but the lives they've touched along the way. These are not just business stories; they are human stories of growth, resilience, creativity, generosity, and leadership.

As you turn the pages ahead, you'll see what entrepreneurship looks like up close. You'll meet people who have failed and started over.

Who have sacrificed time, comfort, and stability in pursuit of a dream. Who have mentored others while building themselves. Who have faced a pandemic, forced closures, uncertainties, and knew that their employees were looking to them for help. They have created more than just jobs; they have empowered their employees to provide for their family, put a roof over their heads, clothes on their back, food on the table, pay for education, vacations, and they've created meaning. And that is the true legacy of an entrepreneur.

The real-life stories you are about to read are transparent, inspiring, and relatable, and will act as a coach for you as you take the most important journey of your life: entrepreneurship.

Let this foreword serve as a reminder: entrepreneurship is not just a business venture. It is a powerful force for good economically, socially, and personally. Entrepreneurs are not just the backbone of our cities; they are the soul. May their stories inspire you to lead with courage, build with intention, and always believe in what's possible.

Finally, I want to share my appreciation to each one of the Entrepreneurs involved in creating this book. Their time and energy towards the project, and their determination to make sure their words would be beneficial to all who read it.

I am proud to be part of this effort, and I thank each one of the entrepreneurs for allowing me into their lives.

> "In any endeavor, it takes ten units of effort for each unit of success until your momentum will generate ten units of success for each unit of effort."
>
> –Peter Remington

BILL BALDWIN

Bill Baldwin is a respected real estate broker, community leader, and advocate for Houston's growth and vitality. As the owner and broker of **Boulevard Realty**, an independent boutique firm serving Houston and Galveston, Bill has built his career on relationships, integrity, and a deep love for his city. Under his leadership, Boulevard has become one of Houston's top-performing firms, recognized not just for its success in sales, but for its commitment to people and community.

A lifelong Houstonian, Bill's work extends far beyond real estate. He co-founded the *Houston Relief Hub* following Hurricane Harvey, coordinating thousands of volunteers and resources for disaster recovery. He has also served as President of the **Houston Heights Association**, co-chaired the Mayor's **Quality of Life Transition Committee**, and currently serves as a City of Houston Planning Commissioner. Through these roles, Bill has been a driving voice for equitable growth, urban livability, and strong neighborhood identity.

Bill believes that every home and development tells a story of progress, purpose, and the people who call Houston home. His vision continues to shape a city that thrives on diversity, innovation, and connection.

An avid reader and fitness enthusiast, he also passionately supports Houston's urban transformation. Ultimately, Bill strives to contribute to a diverse, equitable, and opportunity-rich Houston.

YourBlvd.com
bill@YourBlvd.com

CHAPTER 1

BUILDING A BUSINESS, BUILDING A LIFE: MY JOURNEY AS A REAL ESTATE ENTREPRENEUR

by Bill Baldwin

When people ask me what it means to be an entrepreneur, I often pause, not because I don't have an answer, but because the honest answer is layered. It's not just about starting a business or taking risks. It's about building relationships, remaining a student of your craft, leading with purpose, and deeply investing in the communities you serve.

I've been in real estate for nearly three decades. I didn't grow up dreaming of selling homes, but looking back, I can't imagine doing anything else. Real estate gave me a path, not only to financial success, but also to making a meaningful impact in my city. My story isn't flashy or filled with much drama. It's grounded in the neighborhoods of Houston, in the historic districts I've come to know block by block, and in the lives of thousands of people I've helped navigate one of the most significant decisions they'll ever make.

Relationships Are the Foundation

If I've learned anything in these 28 years, it's that relationships are everything. From the moment I stepped into this business, I knew I couldn't do it alone. You cannot know everything. What you can do is surround yourself with people who know more than you in areas that matter.

Whether it's someone who knows more about termites, construction, permitting, flooding, lending, or title work, each relationship has been a piece of the puzzle that allows me to serve my clients more effectively. I've never been afraid to ask questions. I lean on experts. In turn, that makes me a better resource for the people who count on me. Being a connector of knowledge is just as powerful as being a source of it.

People want to do business with people they know and trust. That trust doesn't happen overnight. It's earned through consistency, presence, and humility.

Never Stop Learning

One of my core beliefs is that you should never stop learning. I have read three newspapers a day for decades: the local paper, the New York Times, and the Wall Street Journal. Even when I'm overseas, in India, Russia, wherever, I find the local paper and keep up with my routine. Knowledge isn't just power; it's preparation.

In the real estate industry, change is constant. Rules evolve, ordinances change, and consumers' behavior shifts. The average homebuyer today is not the same as the one from a decade ago. Many of my buyers now come from out of state, from California or New York, and they arrive with entirely different expectations and assumptions. Staying educated helps me serve them well.

One Phone Number, One Email

I've had the same phone number and the same email address for over 30 years. That's not just a personal quirk, it's a philosophy. I want to be reachable. I want people to know where to find me. In a world that's constantly changing, that kind of stability builds trust.

I receive thousands of emails a day. Sure, many might be useless. But that remaining number, that's where the gold lives. I may ignore a lender's emails for 20 days, but on day 21, there's a rate change that shifts my strategy. You never know which detail will matter, so I stay engaged.

It's Not About Me or You

One of the most important lessons I try to teach new agents, and remind myself of constantly, is this: it's not about me. When I walk into a client's home, it's not my taste or preferences that matter. We are preparing that home for the next buyer, not for the current owner. That means seeing the home through someone else's eyes.

The same applies when helping a buyer. I may not love the house they're excited about. I may prefer a different street or floor plan. But it's not my house - it will be theirs. My job is to understand what they value and help them get it. Perhaps a client is willing to sacrifice closet space for a better backyard. That's their call, not mine. I bought my own house with my preferences in mind. But when I represent someone else, I check my preferences at the door.

Balancing Leadership and Management

As a business owner, you have to wear multiple hats: founder, leader, manager, and mentor. That comes with ego. And ego isn't necessarily a bad thing; you need a little bit of it to push yourself to be the best. I wanted to be a top-producing agent. That ambition fueled me. But when I became the owner of Boulevard Realty in 2008, my role shifted.

Suddenly, it wasn't just about my numbers. It was about the success of 60+ other people. Not everyone wants to be a top producer, and that's okay. Some of my agents value time with their families more than a $40 million sales year. As a manager, I meet them where they are. Some people want to coach Little League, attend church, or enjoy a balanced life. Real estate allows for that flexibility, and it's my job to support whatever version of success they envision.

Scaling with Intention

When I bought the firm, I had already built a strong personal brand as a top-producing agent. But scaling a business required a whole new mindset. I went from being singularly focused on my deals to becoming the "supporter-in-chief" for an entire team.

That transition gave me a more profound sense of purpose. It wasn't just about helping people buy and sell homes. It was about building careers, changing lives, and fostering loyalty. Many of my agents have been with me for decades. My office manager and assistant have been by my side for more than 20 years. That kind of longevity isn't accidental. It's rooted in respect, support, and shared vision.

Mentorship and SLAM

One of the proudest initiatives I've created at Boulevard Realty is our Tuesday SLAM sessions - Sharing, Listening, and Mentoring, unlike traditional sales meetings where leadership talks at the agents, SLAM is agent-driven. They bring the topics, challenges, and solutions. It's real-time collaboration. It's mentoring in action.

We also host a "Listing Laboratory" every Wednesday, where we take a hard look at current listings and analyze them critically. What's working? What isn't? Are the photos as strong as they can be? Is the price aligned with market trends? The goal is constant improvement.

Expertise Sets You Apart

You don't have to know everything in real estate, but you should be an expert in something. Early in my career, I focused on historic districts. I attended Historic Commission meetings, met with city preservation officers, and immersed myself in that niche. Over time, I became a go-to resource for anything historically related in Houston.

After a few years, I became well-versed on new construction and, for the last decade or so, on flood issues. My expertise in flooding, flood risk, and flood regulations has led me to be quoted in articles in The New York Times, The Wall Street Journal, and The Houston Chronicle, as well as numerous periodicals. There have also been numerous appearances on local TV stations, PBS, NPR, and others. Houston's flooding patterns are complex and differ by municipality. I've made it a point to understand those intricacies, and now agents from outside my firm regularly call me for insights. Expertise builds credibility. It builds trust. And trust builds business.

Five Things Every Entrepreneur Should Know

1. **Have realistic expectations.** Whether you're starting a restaurant, real estate firm, or any business, assume your sales will be half of what you think and your expenses will be double. Can you survive like that for two years? If so, you're probably ready.

2. **Find your niche.** You can't be everything to everyone. Focus on something, first-time homebuyers, your neighborhood, a price point. Start narrow and grow wide.

3. **Surround yourself with the right people.** From termite inspectors to attorneys, your network is your knowledge base. Invest in those relationships.

4. **Get up and go to work every day.** Even if you could work from home, don't; being around other professionals sharpens your focus and creates opportunity.

5. **Prepare for good times and bad.** Market crashes, pandemics, interest rate spikes, they're all part of the journey. When you're going through hell, keep going.

Hyperlocal Wins

What sets Boulevard Realty apart is our hyperlocal focus. We're not answering to Wall Street or some CEO in New York. Every decision is based on what's best for Houston. We care about walkability, trees, local parks, small businesses, and schools. We're not just selling homes - we're selling lifestyles.

Yes, buyers can find homes online. They often know the MLS better than we do. But what they don't know is everything else - the culture of the neighborhood, the nuances of city planning, the future of local infrastructure. That's where we bring value.

And yes, I still shop locally. I've never been a big Amazon person. I'd rather walk into a store, talk to the owner, and support the local economy. That philosophy has extended into how I built Boulevard Realty: focused, local, personal.

I'm proud that we've stayed local, unlike many firms that've gone national. Being locally owned means we can make decisions quickly, support our community deeply, and stay connected in ways a franchise never could.

Giving Back and Building Community

I'm out nearly every night, attending community events, fundraisers, or charitable functions. It's not just good business - it's who I am. I believe in cancer research, the arts, parks, preservation, and public education. The people I meet through these causes often become clients. Why? Because we share common values.

When people see me at a gala, they don't just see a real estate broker; they see someone who cares. When they need a Realtor, I'm already top of mind. That combination of purpose and profession has been one of the most fulfilling aspects of my entrepreneurial journey.

Coming Full Circle

My earliest years were spent growing up in Houston. My father coached at the University of Houston and later for the Houston Oilers. In the late 70's, we moved to Huntsville, where I went to high school and college. That small-town upbringing left a mark on me. In my thirties, when I moved back to Houston and settled in The Houston Heights, it reminded me of home - walkable streets, old architecture, and a tight-knit community.

That connection fueled my passion. The Heights embraced me, and I poured myself into it - serving the neighborhood, advocating for quality of life issues, and promoting local businesses. My career has become an extension of that small-town mindset in a big-city world.

Today, I am able to split my time between the urban pulse of Houston and some time at my lake house in Huntsville. The lake house is where I reflect, recharge, and restore. I am not sure if I'll ever fully retire. I love what I do. I love the people I do it with. As long as I can keep making Houston a better place to live, work, and play, I'll keep showing up.

For me, entrepreneurship isn't a job, it's a calling. And I'm just getting started.

DR. JACQUIE BALY

Dr. Jacquie Baly is a nationally recognized public policy expert, academic, philanthropist, and civic leader to helping organizations achieve measurable impact through government and community engagement. As Founder and CEO of **BalyProjects**, she partners with corporations, nonprofits, and government agencies to expand government partnerships and advance impactful policy.

With nearly two decades as a professor at the **University of Houston**, Dr. Baly has mentored countless future leaders. Her public service includes over ten years on the **Governor's University Research Initiative Board**, helping secure $120 million in research funding for Texas universities.

A former **City Planner and Mayor Pro Tem of Sugar Land**, she guided the award-winning development of Sugar Land Town Square. Her leadership portfolio includes board service with the **Brazos River Authority, Baylor Research Advocates for Student Scientists**, and the **American Cancer Society**. She also **chairs the Harris County Women's Commission**, where she leads initiatives that expand economic opportunities for women across the region. In addition, Dr. Baly serves as **Chair** of the **T.W. Davis YMCA's** $16 million Capital Campaign..

Honored with multiple awards including the **Texas Women's Hall of Fame,** has been featured on national networks and publications. Born in St. Croix and raised in Texas, she credits her Caribbean roots for her resilience and lives in Houston with her family.

> "Lead with purpose, rise with resilience, and build a legacy that elevates future generations."

Contact & Social

BalyProjects.com
Linkedin.com/in/dr-jacquie-baly-2b11501
Facebook.com/Jacqueline.Baly.Chaumette
Instagram: @drjacquiebaly
Twitter: @DrJacquieBaly
Media or speaking inquiries: jacquie@BalyProjects.com

CHAPTER 2

FROM BARRIERS
TO BREAKTHROUGHS

by Dr. Jacquie Baly

Success often emerges from the challenges we're brave enough to confront. For many immigrants and entrepreneurs, those challenges become the proving grounds where resilience, creativity, and growth take root. I was only seven when I moved to Texas, accented, curious, and completely immersed in an unfamiliar culture. That moment began a journey filled with unexpected detours that led me through public policy, business, and academia. Along the way, I learned that education, strategic thinking, and an unshakable drive can create opportunities for us and others.

Over the years, I've seen every obstacle as an invitation to learn, evolve, and lead. The very experiences that once made me feel like an outsider now inform how I move through the world. They've become the foundation of my approach, guiding policy discussions, building community partnerships, or mentoring the next generation of changemakers. My goal is to share what I've learned, not as a blueprint but as encouragement for others to chart their bold path forward.

Education: A Bridge to Opportunity

Education is the first key to unlocking opportunity for so many immigrants. That was certainly true for me. Pursuing academic excellence wasn't just a personal ambition; it became a way to create space at the table and invite others in. Earning a doctorate in education and organizational leadership from the University of Southern California gave me the tools to dig deeper into issues I care about, especially equity in education.

My dissertation focused on the barriers facing African American students and the institutional support systems that can help them thrive. That work has informed my 18-year career as a professor at the University of Houston, where mentoring first-generation college students, many of whom are navigating cultural, legal, and academic systems for the first time, has been among the most rewarding aspects of my professional life. Each story reinforces my belief that education isn't just about degrees; it's about empowerment, access, and legacy.

Entrepreneurship: Navigating and Shaping Opportunity

Starting BalyProjects was a leap of faith, and one of the best decisions I've made. It allowed me to blend my background in public policy with business, offering consulting services to government agencies, nonprofits, and corporations on vital issues like economic development, infrastructure, and civic engagement. Entrepreneurship has challenged me to think differently, lead boldly, and find creative solutions in spaces that don't always welcome change.

Being a Black immigrant woman has shaped how I lead. My perspective is informed by the barriers I've overcome and the communities I serve. That dual lens is my greatest asset; it brings work depth, empathy, and urgency. Whether guiding a client through a complex policy issue or helping launch a community-driven initiative, I always bring that experience to the table.

Community Commitment: Professional and Philanthropic

Growing up as an immigrant instilled in me a deep sense of responsibility to show up, to speak out, and to make a difference. That commitment to service has been a throughline in everything I do. It led me to public service and academia and to launch my firm. But just as important, it led me to philanthropy.

From leading major fundraising campaigns to serving on nonprofit boards like the American Cancer Society and YMCA, I've used my platform to drive impact where it matters most. Philanthropy, to me, isn't separate from entrepreneurship. It's an extension of it. It's about using the same strategic thinking that builds a business to build stronger, healthier communities.

Resilience and Leadership: Building a Legacy

Resilience has never been optional. It's been essential. Breaking barriers in academia, leading in civic spaces, and pushing for inclusive policy haven't always been easy, but it's made me a stronger leader. My work with the Harris County Women's Commission, NAWBO, and other civic organizations reflects a commitment to equity, especially for women and immigrants navigating complex systems.

True leadership isn't just about achieving your goals but helping others rise. That's why mentoring young professionals, particularly women of color and immigrant youth, is a non-negotiable part of my work. Whether advising on legislation, teaching in the classroom, or coaching someone through their career pivot, I lead with the belief that strategy, empathy, and courage go hand in hand.

Philanthropy and Impact

Philanthropy has been a cornerstone of my career. I've led multimillion-dollar campaigns, like the $15 million raised for the T.W. Davis YMCA, and directed those efforts toward causes close to my heart, including health equity, education access, and women's empowerment. These experiences have shown me how effective business strategies can fuel lasting change.

When done with intention, philanthropy can be transformative. It's not just about writing checks; it's about creating systems, raising awareness, and building partnerships that change lives. Whether helping fund student scholarships or championing cancer research, my goal remains the same: to ensure that opportunity is not the exception but the norm.

Where Purpose Begins: My Family

My story is one thread in a much larger tapestry woven by generations before me. My parents, immigrants from the West Indies, were trailblazers in every sense of the word. Leaving behind their home in St. Martin/Maarten and the comfort of family and familiarity, they came to the United States in pursuit of the American Dream. They brought with them a tireless work ethic, unwavering values, and a vision for a better future. Their courage laid the foundation for everything I've become. Public service and leadership run deep in my lineage; my Paternal grandfather served as a council member in St. Martin, and today, my cousin serves as the Governor of St. Maarten.. From the Caribbean to Texas, our family has continued the legacy of shaping policy, advocating for our communities, and leaving things better than we found them. It's in our DNA.

That legacy now lives on through my two sons, affectionately known as my #PerfectSons. One earned his MBA from Boston College and now leads as a senior marketing strategist; the other is a Harvard medical student already contributing to nationally recognized research. Watching them thrive as compassionate, driven, and purpose-filled men has been the most rewarding chapter of my life.

They understand that true success means lifting others as you rise. Five years ago, I married my husband, a successful business executive whose partnership has brought new strength and support to this journey. Together, our blended family reflects the power of resilience, grace, and generational impact. Our story is one of progress and purpose built on sacrifice, shaped by service, and committed to paving the way for others across both American and Caribbean communities.

Conclusion: A Call to Action

My story is just one of many. Thousands of immigrant entrepreneurs, educators, and leaders use their voices and talents to build a better future. My hope is that this chapter offers encouragement and a reminder that the path to success isn't always linear. It's paved with setbacks, detours, and moments of doubt but also with breakthroughs, purpose, and progress.

To those forging their own way: invest in your education, lead with integrity, and don't be afraid to take risks. Use your story to power your purpose. In business, policy, or philanthropy, there's room for us to lead, lift others, and leave a legacy that matters.

Each challenge you overcome becomes a building block for someone else's foundation. Your struggles carry wisdom. Your voice, especially when it breaks barriers or speaks truth in difficult spaces, carries the potential to ignite change. You may not always feel seen or heard, but your presence matters. Your persistence matters. What you build, whether it's a classroom, a community program, a startup, or a movement, ripples beyond what you can imagine.

I've learned that success isn't just about what you gain, it's also about what you give. Sharing your resources, your knowledge, and your encouragement creates opportunity for others. And when we rise together, we reshape entire narratives.

So keep going. Keep learning. Surround yourself with people who challenge and uplift you. Step into leadership not just with ambition, but with empathy and a commitment to service. The next generation is watching, and they need to see what's possible.

This is your time to lead boldly, dream fully, and live intentionally. Never forget: the world needs your story, your vision, and your courage to keep moving forward.

The two most important days of your life are
the day you were born…
And the day you discovered why!

–Mark Twain

LARY BARTON

Lary Barton is committed to excellence. He listens and guides his buyers to a purchase that suits their needs and assists sellers in hitting the mark with pricing. Lary has a proven record of over 40 years of exceptional customer service and knows the client always comes first. He relishes the opportunity to employ his impressive sales experience to achieve the goal of making his client's dreams come true. As a native of Houston, Lary is an expert in the Houston area home market. Whether you or someone you know is looking for a single-family home or a high-rise, Lary can open the right doors today. Lary believes that honesty, integrity, humility, and an eye for detail are qualities that make him an asset to all his clients at Martha Turner Sotheby's International Realty. Trust is the foundation for any great relationship, so establishing trust is key to Lary's sales approach. He helps with the staging of his listings, recognizing the importance of presentation in making the sale.

Lary holds a BBA in Business and Organizational Behavioral Management from The University of Houston. His volunteer activities include serving on the Boards of Healthcare for the Homeless Houston, Bering Omega Community Services, Avenue 360, Open Gate Homeless Ministries, serving as Board Chair of the Trustees, Board member for HeartGift, and Advisory Board for 4th Wall Theater.

Martha Turner Sotheby's International Realty
SothebysHomes.com
LaryBartonRealtor.com
Lary.barton@sothebys.realty
Lary Barton Realtor - YouTube
Instagram: @LaryBartonRealtor

CHAPTER 3

WAKING UP WITH PURPOSE

by Lary Barton

There's a particular magic in waking up every morning with a sense of purpose, and lately, I've found myself smiling before I even pour my first cup of coffee. It's not because everything in life suddenly became easy or perfect. It's because I finally found the work that makes my soul hum, the people who challenge and support me, and a mission that feels bigger than me.

But it didn't start with clarity. It started with a nudge.

I'd spent over four decades in outsourcing, high-level sales, operations, and strategy. It was a career I loved and one that had given me plenty of wins and friends. But as companies changed and the industry evolved, I could feel a shift inside me. It was subtle at first: a discomfort, a lack of spark. And then, life started nudging me harder.

A friend called and said they'd just gotten their real estate license. On the very same day, I walked out of a session with my life coach (John Vincent), who had asked me, bluntly, "What's next?"

That was the ding. The sign. The intersection between intuition and opportunity. And I paid attention.

The Mindset to Reinvent

Starting something new, especially after 41 years in another field, is not for the faint of heart. But I knew two things: I had an itch that wouldn't go away, and I still had more to give.

Mindset, in moments like this, is everything.

So I decided to treat this as a calling, not a pivot. I threw myself into learning, absorbing everything I could about real estate. I partnered with others in the industry and studied new tools, cold calling software, video messaging, and client retention strategies. I didn't pretend to know it all. I embraced the role of student and, like most every serious decision I have ever made, I consulted my subject matter experts and sifted all the information in the Lary blender to find my solution.

And even when it was hard, especially during COVID, when cold calls often led to silence, I didn't let frustration win. I held onto one truth: I was made to connect. If I kept showing up with the right attitude, the results would come.

They did. Slowly. Then all at once.

The Confidence to Begin Again

When I showed up to my first client meetings, I didn't hide that I was new to real estate. But I also didn't shrink back. I had confidence, not just because of the sales skills I'd honed over the years, but because I'd done the internal work to believe in myself.

Confidence isn't about being loud. It's about being grounded.

I wasn't always this sure of myself. Early in life, I had what you might call bravado. But it was a mask. I'd put on a show of confidence without really feeling it deep down. Then something difficult happened in my life, a wake-up call. I walked into my life coach's office and said, "I don't care how long it takes or how much it costs. I want to become the best version of me."

Years later, I'm still on that journey. Still learning. Still growing. But what's different now is that my confidence is rooted. There's a foundation. And on that foundation, I can build not only a career, but a life that supports others, too.

Embracing Vulnerability: The Path to Deeper Connections and Personal Growth

Vulnerability is often perceived as a weakness, but in reality, it is a powerful strength that can lead to profound personal growth and deeper connections with others. Embracing vulnerability means allowing ourselves to be open and honest about our feelings, fears, and experiences. Here's how this openness can transform our lives:

Brené Brown, a renowned researcher and author, has extensively studied vulnerability and its impact on our lives. One of her most powerful quotes on the subject is:

> "Vulnerability is the birthplace of love, belonging, joy, courage, empathy, and creativity. It is the source of hope, empathy, accountability, and authenticity."

This quote encapsulates the essence of vulnerability and its transformative power. By embracing vulnerability, we open ourselves to a richer, more fulfilling life filled with meaningful connections and personal growth.

Embracing vulnerability is a powerful step towards deeper connections and personal growth. By allowing ourselves to be open and authentic, we create a richer, more fulfilling life for ourselves and those around us.

Paying It Forward

Let me tell you a story.

One day, an agent couldn't make a house showing and asked me to fill in. I drove out to Memorial, not thinking much of it. When I got there, I met a couple and their ten-year-old daughter. As the mother and daughter explored the house with their agent, the man turned to me and asked how long I'd been in real estate.

I told him: just about a year.

He paused, then shared that he'd just been let go from his role as an attorney in the medical industry. He said, "I've got money, but my daughter needs to see me going to work every day. She needs to see what it means to show up." I gave him the number of my life coach, Dawn Nelson (yes, I have two life coaches, it takes a big village with me). A year later, I ran into him again. He was glowing. Smiling. He'd started his own firm and was thriving. He thanked me.

But here's the thing, I didn't do anything magical. I just shared my story. I passed along a name, a lifeline, and it made a difference.

We all carry stories that can be a lifeboat for someone else. When we hide our pain or downplay our victories, we rob others of the chance to feel seen, to believe something new is possible for them. That's why I talk openly. That's why I always do my best to pay it forward.

The Connector Philosophy

People often call me "the connector." I like that. It's accurate.

Back in my outsourcing days, I'd say, "Need a haircut? A roofer? A new car? Call me." I'd connect people without expecting anything in return. But deep down, I believed one day they'd call for what I did do, IT solutions. I wanted to be top of mind, not just for business, but because I love helping.

That habit carried into real estate. Now, whether someone's looking for a home, a dentist, or a publisher (yes, I refer people to Elite Online Publishing all the time), I want to be the person they trust.

It starts with listening.

My dad used to tell me, "Lary, if you just shut up long enough, everyone's got a story." So I try to do that, shut up, lean in, and let people tell me who they are. Then I help them take the next step, even if that next step has nothing to do with me.

Because when you really love people, you want to see them win.

Self-Work Is the Secret Sauce

People assume I'm naturally confident or outgoing. But as I've said, this didn't come out of nowhere. It came from work. Deep, consistent, sometimes uncomfortable self-work.

If you want to live a rich life, one that overflows into others, you've got to know who you are. Not who you think you are. Not who others expect you to be. But the real you.

For me, God, therapy, and coaching helped fill the bottomless bucket that was my self-esteem. It didn't matter how many cars I drove or how many deals I closed; without that inner work, none of it stuck. I could hear compliments, but they'd slip right through. Now? The bucket still has a few pinholes. I'm human. But it holds water. It holds true.

I can believe the good things people say about me. And I can pass that belief on to others.

Keep Moving Forward

The biggest shift in my mindset, what's helped me weather the tough days and keep growing, is this: I don't stop. I don't ruminate. I move forward.

Things go wrong. Plans fall apart. Phones break. (Right, Melanie?) But I've learned that resilience isn't about being unshakable. It's about how fast you return to center. It's about laughing even when the day has gone sideways. It's about choosing to keep moving, because momentum builds more than perfection ever will.

I've seen this in my life, and I've seen it in others. Some of the people I most admire are the ones who've faced massive challenges and kept smiling. Kept giving. Kept rising.

And I'd rather be around people like that than any billionaire or big shot.

Attracting Abundance

Here's something I believe with my whole heart: when you live in joy, abundance follows.

It's not a gimmick. It's not wishful thinking. It's energy.

When you're stressed, when you feel desperate, people can feel it. Doors close. Opportunities dry up. But when you're genuinely enjoying your life, when you're present, grateful, and helping others, abundance finds you.

My dad used to say that success isn't measured by what you take, but by what you give. He said true fulfillment is watching someone else succeed and knowing, in your heart, that you had a quiet hand in it.

That's the kind of wealth I'm after. Not just commissions or status, but a ripple effect that lasts.

The Power of Community

One of the most profound lessons I've learned is the importance of community. When I transitioned into real estate, I didn't do it alone. I had mentors, colleagues, and friends who supported me every step of the way. They shared their knowledge, offered encouragement, and celebrated my successes. It's important who you choose to share with; not everyone will be there to celebrate you. For as long as I can remember, I have sought the advice of those in my trust circle. I take their input, put it in the Lary blender, and come up with an idea or answer that incorporates all the ideas that went into the blender. This sense of community has been invaluable. It reminds me that we are all interconnected and that our collective strength can overcome any obstacle.

Building a community isn't just about networking; it's about creating genuine relationships based on trust and mutual respect. It's about being there for each other, not just in times of success, but also in times of struggle. When we lift each other up, we create a ripple effect that extends far beyond our immediate circle.

The Role of Gratitude
Practical Ways to Cultivate Gratitude

1. **Gratitude Journaling**: Keep a daily journal where you write down three things you are grateful for. This simple practice can help you focus on the positive aspects of your day.

2. **Expressing Thanks**: Take the time to thank the people in your life who have made a difference. A heartfelt note or a simple thank you can go a long way.

3. **Mindful Moments**: Take a few moments each day to pause and reflect on the things you are grateful for. This can be done during meditation, while taking a walk, or even during a quiet moment at work.

4. **Gratitude Rituals**: Incorporate gratitude into your daily routines. For example, you could start your day by thinking of something you are grateful for or end your day by reflecting on the positive moments.

By integrating gratitude into our daily lives, we can create a foundation of positivity and abundance that supports our personal and professional growth. It's a simple yet profound practice that can transform our mindset and our lives.

Your Story Has Power

If there's one thing I hope you take from this chapter, it's that your story matters.

Whatever you've walked through, your successes, your failures, your quiet reinventions, it's not just about you. It's a blueprint for someone else's breakthrough.

So, tell it.

Better yet, live it fully. Smile more often. Pay attention to the nudges. Share your lessons. And believe, really believe, that your next chapter can be your best chapter.

I know mine is.

The pain endured while making a vision happen
Doesn't last nearly as long as the
Pain endured knowing that you quit!

–Peter C. Remington

STEVEN LAWRENCE BIEGEL, AIA, LEED AP

Steven Lawrence Biegel, AIA, LEED AP, is a distinguished architect, CEO, and thought leader with more than 45 years of experience shaping the built environment through innovation and strategic design. A registered architect and member of the American Institute of Architects, he has overseen thousands of projects nationwide, from major federal renovations to mixed-use and ground-up developments.

Steven currently serves as Director of Architecture at PLACE Designers in Round Rock, Texas, and CEO of The Matrix Design Companies, a national network of architecture and engineering firms operating across multiple states. His expertise spans sustainable design, adaptive reuse, and federal procurement, leading multidisciplinary teams that blend creativity with technical excellence.

Before founding Matrix, Steven held senior roles at URS Greiner, Einhorn Yaffee Prescott, and the National Institute of Building Sciences. He is NCARB certified, LEED accredited, and the author of Profit by Design, a guide for running profitable A/E practices. He also contributed to the Encyclopedia of Architecture, Design & Construction.

A lifelong advocate for the profession, Steven has served on national AIA committees and local boards. A graduate of Syracuse University, he pursued advanced studies at the University of Virginia and George Washington University. Outside of work, he enjoys sailing, art, music, and public speaking.

sbiegel@placedesigners.com
sbiegel@broadviewcorp.com
sbiegel@matrixdesigncompanies.com

CHAPTER 4

BUILDING BEYOND THE BLUEPRINT: HOW VISION AND STRATEGY DRIVE SUCCESS

by Steven Lawrence Biegel, AIA, LEED AP

The economics of growth in a professional services corporation can be complex. The corporate mission must be clear and well-understood by both owners and decision-makers.

As an architect licensed 46 years ago, I remember entering the profession both self-confident and befuddled. In those early days, I wondered: "Why aren't clients lining up at my door with projects in hand?" I had passed the licensing exam on my first try in 1979 and viewed myself as the second coming of Frank Lloyd Wright, Louis Kahn, or Alvar Aalto. Standing at the threshold of my career, I asked myself: How do I practice architecture and become successful? I prayed and sought spiritual guidance.

I had already won the Reynolds Aluminum Prize for Architectural Students at Syracuse University and had been elected Student Vice President of the American Institute of Architects (AIA), a role that brought me to Washington, D.C. for two years. Those experiences were truly life-changing. Serving on the AIA National Board of Directors gave me an education that could never be replicated in a classroom. During those two years, I participated in countless committees and had the rare opportunity to meet icons like I.M. Pei, Richard Meier, Frank Gehry, Sir Norman Foster, Moshe Safdie, and E. Fay Jones. My aspiration and motivation were to become like them.

Shortly after completing my degree, the AIA invited me to return to Washington as a lobbyist for its Government Affairs Division. Having already served in the organization, I was a known commodity and was thrilled to serve my profession on Capitol Hill. I had no idea how to merge an architectural education with politics, yet I knew someone else was in control of my destiny, and my career was being shaped in ways I never anticipated.

When my architectural license finally arrived in February 1980, I made what I now see as my first mistake: I rented office space in Occoquan, Virginia, and proudly hung a sign reading "Steven Biegel, Architect." My glass-front office was beautiful, but the phone didn't ring. This was before the internet, and phones were still tethered by cords. Despite being the only architect in town, I went eight months without a single job. It was demoralizing. Eventually, I landed my first commission: renovating Marine Corps barracks at the FBI Academy in Quantico, Virginia. It wasn't glamorous work, closets and toilet rooms, but it was a start.

Soon after, I was named Director of Program Planning for the National Institute of Building Sciences, a Congressionally Chartered organization backed by senior industry leaders. That role gave me incredible exposure to the wider construction industry. Executives from Monsanto, DuPont, USG, the National Home Builders Association, and many more came through our offices regularly. It was a crash course in construction economics, management, and government regulation.

Armed with that knowledge and my architectural education from Syracuse, I made my second big mistake: opening another small architectural office, this time in Warrenton, Virginia. Once again,

I had no clients and no credit line. It was hand-to-mouth survival. Friends warned me that architecture was a fringe business, vulnerable to every economic downturn. I ignored them. I had a fire in my belly and faith in my destiny.

It wasn't long before I realized that owning a small design firm was far less satisfying than I had imagined. The solution was to study how larger firms grew and sustained profitable operations. That led me to explore real business strategies, things never taught in architecture school. I studied the mega-firms and their growth strategies. The most enlightening lesson was that architects don't sell design talent; they sell time. In 2003, I published my findings in a book called *Profit by Design*, aimed at students and young professionals to help them avoid the same missteps I made. In 2023, I released a second edition.

Here is the essence of what I've learned:

Business Growth Strategies

1. **Market Penetration**, Increase market share in existing markets through targeted marketing, competitive pricing, and superior customer service. Enhancing product visibility, running promotions, and optimizing distribution channels can deepen customer loyalty and steal market share from competitors. This strategy works best when the market is not yet saturated, and the company already has a solid presence.

2. **Market Development**, Enter new markets using existing products to access untapped customer segments. Expansion can occur across geographic regions, demographics, or new use-cases. This approach is ideal for businesses that have maxed out their current market but believe their product or service has broader applicability beyond their current clientele.

3. **Product Development**, Innovate or improve your products to better address the evolving needs of your existing customer

base. This might involve adding new features, improving performance, enhancing aesthetics, or bundling with services. This strategy deepens customer engagement while defending your market share from more innovative competitors.

4. **Diversification**, Introduce entirely new products or services into new or unrelated markets. This strategy spreads business risk by reducing dependence on any single industry or customer base. Successful diversification requires research, planning, and alignment with the company's broader vision and capabilities to ensure long-term viability.

5. **Acquisition and Mergers**, Accelerate growth by purchasing or merging with other businesses to quickly scale operations, enter new markets, or acquire talent and intellectual property. While potentially transformative, this strategy requires due diligence and integration planning to avoid cultural clashes and ensure operational alignment.

6. **Partnerships and Alliances**, Form strategic collaborations with other businesses to leverage complementary strengths. These alliances can drive innovation, expand market reach, share risks, and improve resource utilization. When structured thoughtfully, partnerships offer mutual benefits that might not be achievable independently.

7. **Franchising**, Scale a proven business model by allowing other entrepreneurs to replicate your operations under your brand. Franchising enables rapid geographic growth with lower capital investment from the parent company, while providing local operators the chance to succeed using established systems and brand recognition.

8. **Digital Transformation**, Adopt technologies such as cloud computing, CRM platforms, data analytics, and e-commerce to enhance operational efficiency and customer engagement. Digital transformation not only modernizes the business but

can create new revenue streams, improve agility, and foster innovation at every level.

9. **Customer Relationship Management (CRM)**, Build lasting relationships with customers through personalized interactions, loyalty programs, and responsive service. CRM tools allow businesses to analyze customer behavior and preferences, enabling them to anticipate needs, tailor offerings, and drive repeat business and referrals.

10. **Sustainability Practices**, Incorporate environmentally and socially responsible policies that resonate with today's conscious consumers. Implementing green processes, reducing waste, and supporting community initiatives can enhance brand image, attract like-minded customers, and even open doors to new regulatory or grant opportunities.

11. **Continuous Improvement and Innovation**, Regularly analyze business performance, solicit feedback, and experiment with new ideas. A culture of continuous improvement keeps the organization adaptive and resilient, ensuring that products, services, and internal processes remain aligned with market demands and operational excellence.

12. **Talent Development**, Invest in employees through ongoing training, mentorship, and leadership programs. Continuous development not only boosts morale and productivity but also increases retention. People often leave organizations when growth stagnates. Developing your team ensures they grow with you and drive the company's long-term success.

By utilizing some or all of these strategies, businesses lay down the foundational structure that supports goal achievement, fosters creativity, enhances collaboration, drives revenue, and positions themselves for sustainable, long-term success. When I applied these many points to my architectural practice, it became obvious that success is derived from a combination of good design and great management.

It took years to integrate design skills with business sense. When the process became replicable and efficient, I began purchasing small architectural firms and rolling them together into a larger, more profitable enterprise. The fun began when I realized that acquiring existing firms meant buying established portfolios, client base, and talented staff. When we shave the inefficiency out of an existing firm and consolidate overhead, resources become available to embark on specialties and new skill sets. New insights evolved.

Business Insights

1. **Niche Specialization** — Focus on a particular segment of the market to develop deep expertise and set your business apart from generalists. Whether serving a specific industry or customer demographic, specialization creates brand clarity, attracts clients with targeted needs, and allows you to command premium pricing based on your reputation and tailored value.

2. **Green Design** — Embrace eco-conscious practices to align with global sustainability trends and evolving consumer preferences. Businesses that minimize their environmental impact not only contribute to a healthier planet but also benefit from cost savings, regulatory incentives, and brand loyalty among increasingly conscientious customers.

3. **Collaborative Approach** — Foster partnerships with other professionals or organizations to leverage collective strengths. Collaboration enhances problem-solving, accelerates innovation, and improves project outcomes by bringing diverse perspectives to the table. A culture of collaboration builds stronger networks and more resilient, team-oriented operations.

4. **Technology Integration** — Implement digital tools that streamline processes, enhance communication, and improve

service delivery. Whether through automation, data analytics, or immersive customer interfaces, integrating technology helps businesses stay competitive, reduce operational inefficiencies, and elevate the overall client experience.

5. **Client Engagement** — Develop authentic, proactive communication strategies that keep clients informed and involved. High levels of engagement foster loyalty, enable timely issue resolution, and turn satisfied clients into brand advocates. Active listening and responsiveness ensure your offerings align with evolving customer needs.

6. **Diversified Services** — Broaden your service portfolio to meet a wider array of client needs under one roof. This not only adds value for customers but also provides multiple income streams, protecting your business from downturns in any single area and allowing for strategic cross-selling.

7. **Marketing and Branding** — Create a cohesive and compelling brand identity that resonates with your audience. Effective branding tells your story, reflects your values, and builds emotional connections. Strategic marketing amplifies visibility, builds trust, and differentiates your business in a crowded market.

8. **Networking and Community Involvement** — Engage consistently in industry associations, local organizations, and events to build meaningful relationships. These efforts increase credibility, provide access to referrals and insights, and position your business as a trusted, active member of its ecosystem.

9. **Lifelong Learning** — Encourage continuous personal and professional development to stay ahead of the curve. Investing in learning fosters adaptability, sharpens skills, and drives innovation. Teams that embrace growth mindsets are more agile, collaborative, and equipped to navigate changing landscapes.

10. **Client-Centric Flexibility** — Offer adaptable solutions and services that reflect your clients' dynamic needs. The ability to pivot quickly in response to feedback, budget changes, or evolving objectives makes your business more resilient and client-focused, resulting in long-term relationships and repeat opportunities.
11. **Cost Management** — Maintain a disciplined, transparent approach to budgeting and financial oversight. By actively monitoring costs and providing clients with clear, honest projections, you reinforce trust and avoid surprises that can derail projects or damage reputations.
12. **Feedback and Evaluation** — Establish formal mechanisms to gather feedback and analyze performance. Constructive input from clients and stakeholders helps refine services, identify blind spots, and ensure continuous improvement. Regular evaluation leads to smarter decisions and stronger customer satisfaction.

Comparing Growth by Acquisition vs. Organic Growth

1. **Definition** — Acquisition involves buying firms to grow quickly by leveraging their client base, workforce, and market reach. Organic growth, in contrast, expands the business from within through investments in marketing, staffing, and operations.
2. **Speed** — Acquisition provides a fast track to scale but often comes with significant change management. Organic growth is more gradual, offering time to refine systems and build culture without disruption.
3. **Risk** — Acquisition can introduce cultural clashes, integration hurdles, or hidden liabilities. In contrast, organic growth avoids these shocks but may be vulnerable to market saturation or slow uptake in competitive sectors.

4. **Cost** — Acquiring another firm typically requires major upfront investment or financing. Organic growth spreads costs over time and often leverages existing resources, but may take longer to show returns.

5. **Control** — Organic growth allows for consistent brand and cultural evolution. Acquisitions may challenge leadership with the need to harmonize differing processes, values, or management styles, diluting cohesion.

6. **Customer Relations** — Organic growth builds loyalty over time through consistent service and communication. Acquisition risks alienating existing clients if changes in personnel, policy, or service quality occur.

7. **Innovation** — Organically grown firms tend to be more agile and innovative due to their cohesive teams and culture. Acquisitions may slow innovation while new systems and hierarchies are being integrated, potentially stifling creativity during transition periods.

Now, more than 46 years after becoming licensed, I can say this with certainty: if growth is your goal, consider acquisition. Hiring one person at a time is too slow. Acquiring a firm gives you immediate access to new markets and cross-selling opportunities across project types and geographies.

Today, with more than 3,000 completed structures behind me, I credit my success to a combination of disciplined learning, strategic thinking, and the spiritual awareness that each day brings something new. Ultimately, those daily gifts and a belief in something greater have guided me to where I am today.

MATT BRICE

Matt Brice is the Founder and CEO of Federal American Grill, a celebrated restaurant brand known for its elevated hospitality, classic American cuisine, and unwavering commitment to community. A passionate entrepreneur and industry trailblazer, Matt built his company on the belief that people come first, a philosophy that helped him and his team not only survive but thrive through unprecedented challenges, including the COVID-19 pandemic.

With more than two decades in the restaurant business, Matt's journey from dishwasher to visionary leader is a testament to grit, grace, and growth. His hands-on leadership style and authentic approach have earned him the respect of his peers, the loyalty of his staff, and the support of the communities he serves.

Today, Matt continues to expand the Federal American Grill brand while mentoring the next generation of restaurateurs. He is a sought-after speaker on topics such as resilience, leadership, and company culture, and remains deeply committed to creating meaningful experiences, both at the table and beyond.

Matt lives in Texas with his family and enjoys golf, great bourbon, and any opportunity to lift others up.

Federal American Grill
TheFederalGrill.com

CHAPTER 5

A CRASH COURSE IN RESILIENCE: OPENING A RESTAURANT IN THE MIDDLE OF A PANDEMIC

**by Matt Brice,
CEO and Founder, Federal American Grill**

On **March 3,** 2020, the Hedwig Village location of Federal American Grill opened its doors with high hopes. We had poured our hearts, souls, and resources into making this third location a reality. The team was energized, the menu was ready, and the dining room buzzed with the energy of new beginnings.

Little did we know that just fourteen days later, those very same doors would be closed.

The global COVID-19 pandemic wasn't just a news headline anymore; it had landed squarely on our doorstep, bringing with it an overwhelming sense of uncertainty. The city of Houston, like so many others, announced mandatory shutdowns. Restaurants were ordered to close their dining rooms. The business we had built over the years, and the new one we had barely begun, was suddenly in jeopardy.

The Initial Shock

The first few days after the shutdown were surreal. I remember sitting alone in the empty dining room at Hedwig Village, staring at the rows of untouched tables and chairs. We had barely gotten started, just two weeks in, and already we were facing the possibility that this new venture might not survive.

We had opened Federal American Grill with a deep belief in the power of community and a passion for hospitality. It wasn't just about food; it was about connection. And now, connections were being severed everywhere.

But in that moment, a simple truth became clear: this wasn't the time to focus on what we couldn't do. It was time to focus on what we could.

Pivoting to Possibility

As a leader, I quickly realized our team was looking to us for answers, and more importantly, for hope. We didn't have a playbook for navigating a global pandemic, but we did know one thing: the only way we would get through this was together.

Within days, we pivoted to a takeout and delivery model. It wasn't glamorous, and it certainly wasn't what we had envisioned for Hedwig Village's first month of operations. But it was a lifeline, both for the business and for our team.

We turned our parking lot into a curbside pickup operation. Our bartenders started batching cocktails to-go. Chefs who had once focused on elegant plating now packed meals into takeout containers with care and precision. Every single person pitched in, no matter their role.

That experience bonded us in a way we could have never anticipated. Adversity stripped away titles and egos. We were simply people trying to support one another and serve our community.

Finding Strength in the Community

What happened next was nothing short of humbling.

Customers, many of whom we barely knew yet, showed up. They ordered meals. They bought gift cards. They left generous tips to help support our staff. They wrote notes of encouragement on receipts and on social media.

The Federal American Grill wasn't just a restaurant to them; it was a piece of the community they didn't want to lose.

We realized that being vulnerable and transparent about our challenges wasn't a weakness. It was an opportunity to deepen trust. We began communicating openly with our guests about what we were facing and how they could help. And help they did.

The community's support fueled us through some of the darkest days of the pandemic. It reminded us that leadership isn't about standing above the storm, it's about standing in it, shoulder to shoulder with your people.

We were almost four weeks into the shutdown when our team made a critical decision: we had to open. We needed to work, not just for our finances, but for our mental health. And our community needed a place to feel normal again.

I made the decision to reopen the Hedwig Village location of Federal American Grill, against government orders, not out of defiance, but out of a deep sense of responsibility to our team and community. We implemented every safety protocol imaginable, from distanced seating to contactless everything.

The response was overwhelming. Guests were grateful. Our staff was empowered. The restaurant thrived.

Word spread quickly. Before long, the governor's office reached out. They asked for our exact playbook on how to reopen safely, and used it as a model to help guide the reopening of restaurants across the entire state. It was one of the proudest and most surreal moments of my career.

Lessons in Leadership

Looking back, COVID taught us more about leadership than any business class or book ever could. Among the key lessons:

- **Adaptability is everything.** We had to reinvent our operations on the fly, often daily, as regulations and conditions changed.
- **People come first.** Taking care of our team emotionally and financially was critical. We created an employee relief fund and found creative ways to keep as many people employed as possible.
- **Transparency builds trust.** Whether communicating with employees about the realities of the situation or being honest with our guests, open communication became a pillar of our culture.
- **Community matters.** A restaurant isn't just a place to eat, it's a hub for human connection. Nurturing that sense of community is one of the most valuable investments any business can make.

Coming Out Stronger

Eventually, the lockdowns eased. Slowly but surely, the spirit of socializing returned to our great state, this time with a deeper sense of gratitude.

Ironically, the restaurant that began under the shadow of COVID became one of our most resilient and connected locations. The relationships forged through struggle made us stronger, as a team and as a brand.

Federal American Grill didn't just survive the pandemic; it grew. And we grew stronger as a team and as leaders in our community.

When people ask me today what I'm most proud of in my career, the answer isn't about the number of locations we've opened or the accolades we've received. It's that in one of the hardest times imaginable, we showed up for each other. We stayed true to who we were. And we came through it, together.

CHARLES CLARK

Charles Clark, Owner, **Brasserie 19** A small-town Louisiana native with a passion for bold flavors and generous hospitality, Charles Clark became one of Houston's most enduring culinary personalities and restaurateurs with his restaurant Ibiza Food & Wine Bar. At the heart of his current work is **Brasserie 19**, the iconic River Oaks dining destination where rosés are de rigueur in the summer, robust reds are poured all year long, and French brasserie classics are served with unmistakable flair.

Clark's approach to hospitality can best be described as intentional. On any given night, you'll find him walking the floor at **Brasserie 19**, greeting regulars by name, checking in on tables, and ensuring every guest feels like the star of the show. With its crisp white interior, high-energy crowd, and a wine list that encourages bottle service at every table, **Brasserie 19** isn't just a restaurant; it's Houston's ultimate see-and-be-seen experience. And Clark is at the center of it all.

Born in DeQuincy, Louisiana, Clark grew up surrounded by culinary tradition, family crab boils, homemade boudin, and Sunday pot roasts were staples. He entered the restaurant world at a young age, working front-of-house roles before embarking on a backpacking trip across Europe and eventually settling in Marbella, Spain. His travels through Morocco, France, the Basque Country, and Greece continue to inspire his work to this day. After enrolling in culinary school in the late '90s, he jumped headfirst into the kitchen and never looked back.

With an appearance on *Iron Chef America*, Charles Clark is a true ambassador for refined yet approachable cuisine, whether he's racing cars or relaxing with a film noir and a great bottle of wine, he lives life as richly as he cooks.

CHAPTER 6

WHERE PURPOSE MEETS THE PLATE

by Charles Clark

Entrepreneurship is more than a career path; it is a calling, a journey fueled by passion, resilience, and an unwavering commitment toward growth. It isn't about suits and spreadsheets or glamorous launch parties. It's about grit. It's about vision. It's about standing in the fire, sometimes literally, and refusing to back down when things get hard. My name is Charles Clark, and my entrepreneurial journey began not in a boardroom or with a business plan, but in the small town of DeQuincy, Louisiana. It was there, starting at just 10 years old, that I learned to hunt and fish. I was taught how to butcher the game and clean the fish. Then came pig roasts, crawfish boils, and other Southern festivities, where I discovered my passion for cooking and gained a glimpse into what would become my life's work.

At that young age, I didn't know I was laying the groundwork for a lifelong journey in hospitality. I didn't grow up dreaming of owning restaurants or managing a hospitality empire. What I knew was that I loved the act of cooking, the transformation of ingredients into experiences. That love carried me through my teenage years, and by

17, I knew this wasn't just a pastime. It was a purpose. It wasn't about feeding people; it was about creating joy, bringing people together, and telling stories through food.

That passion led me to Dallas, Texas, where I was fortunate to train under some of the most influential chefs of their time, including Dean Fearing at The Mansion on Turtle Creek and Stephen Pyles at Star Canyon. These weren't just jobs; they were formative years that shaped my work ethic and sense of excellence. Under their guidance, I didn't just learn how to cook; I learned discipline. I learned that every plate matters. I learned that consistency is not an act but a habit, and that details, the smallest ones, are what elevate good to great.

But I knew that to grow beyond my surroundings, I needed broader exposure. So, I took a leap and went abroad to study food not just as a technique, but as a culture. I traveled throughout Europe, immersing myself in the kitchens of France, the hills of Tuscany, and the bustling tapas bars of Spain. I wasn't just sampling dishes, I was absorbing philosophy, studying heritage, and watching how food was woven into everyday life. That experience cracked something open in me. I saw that food was more than nourishment; it was identity, celebration, memory. That expanded vision forever changed how I would approach the restaurant world.

When I returned to the U.S., I decided to pursue formal education at the Art Institute of Houston's Culinary School. I wanted to validate my knowledge, refine my skills, and challenge myself in a rigorous environment. I graduated at the top of my class in 1996, a milestone that confirmed I wasn't just passionate about food; I was capable of mastering the craft at a high level. More importantly, I had the tools to turn my dream into a thriving enterprise.

By 2001, I was ready to make the leap into entrepreneurship. Alongside my business partner, Grant Cooper, we opened Ibiza Food

& Wine Bar in Midtown Houston. At the time, Midtown was still developing, and many questioned whether it was the right place for a Mediterranean concept. But we had a clear vision, world-class food in a stylish yet accessible setting, anchored by a wine program that made fine bottles approachable and affordable. Rather than inflate prices for prestige, we priced wines just slightly above retail, which allowed our guests to explore more, enjoy more, and return more often.

And they did.

Ibiza wasn't just a successful restaurant; it was a phenomenon. We weren't just serving meals; we were creating memories. People came for birthdays, for engagements, for Tuesdays that needed to feel like Fridays. That's when I realized that we weren't just building a restaurant, we were building a community hub. And that experience became the springboard for what would become a growing restaurant group in Houston.

Over the years, we expanded with concepts like Brasserie 19, Coppa Osteria, Punk's Simple Southern Food, SaltAir Seafood Kitchen, and The Dunlavy. Each restaurant had its own identity, its own soul. But the common thread was always quality, quality of food, quality of service, quality of environment. We built places where people felt special, where details mattered, and where hospitality wasn't a department; it was a way of life.

But make no mistake, entrepreneurship is never a straight line. For all the highlights, there were just as many moments of confusion, risk, and recalibration. Not every concept hit the mark. There were times we misjudged a location, overestimated a trend, or simply failed to connect with our guests. But here's the thing: failure isn't fatal if you learn from it. Every loss has been a lesson. Every setback has strengthened my resilience. That's the thing about being an entrepreneur: you're never done learning. You evolve or you get left behind.

In early 2022, my business partnership with Grant came to an amicable end. After years of collaboration, we decided to go our separate ways, and I took full ownership of Brasserie 19. That was a turning point. For the first time in years, I had total control over a concept that was mine to refine, reshape, and reimagine.

And I went all in.

I became more hands-on than ever before, reworking the menu, reinvesting in the staff, and reimagining the guest experience. I walked the floor every day. I listened. I asked questions. I sat at the bar and observed. We elevated the wine program, polished the service, and leaned into what made Brasserie 19 special in the first place: energy, elegance, and warmth. The results were tangible. Sales rose by 12 to 13 percent in the first year alone. But more than the numbers, I felt a shift in the atmosphere. The restaurant buzzed with new energy. People weren't just dining, they were experiencing something meaningful.

For me, entrepreneurship isn't about profit. It's about purpose. It's about building something that reflects your values, your vision, and your voice. And one of the values I hold most dear is mentorship. Throughout my career, I've made it a priority to invest in people. I've mentored line cooks who became executive chefs, servers who became general managers, and aspiring restaurateurs who went on to build empires of their own. Nothing fills me with more pride than seeing someone I once trained rise to greatness. That's the ripple effect of leadership: you lift others as you climb.

I believe mentorship is a responsibility, not a luxury. If you've walked the path, it's your job to light the way for others. I always tell young entrepreneurs: Learn everything you can, then teach it forward. Be generous with your wisdom. Don't hoard what you've learned; share it, expand it, let it evolve in someone else's hands.

And here's another truth: Leadership starts with culture. I don't run my restaurant with a rulebook; I run it with values. At Brasserie 19, hospitality isn't a strategy; it's a heartbeat. When a guest walks through our door, we don't just serve them, we welcome them into our world. That requires a team that believes in excellence, empathy, and going the extra mile. That belief system starts at the top. You can't expect your staff to care deeply if you don't lead with heart.

Of course, none of this has come easy. The restaurant business is demanding. It can be brutal at times, emotionally, physically, and financially. There have been sleepless nights, missed holidays, and moments where I questioned everything. But every time I've hit a wall, I've asked myself: Why did I start? And the answer always brings me back to that 10-year-old boy in DeQuincy, skinning fish and stoking fires, dreaming not of Michelin stars or accolades, but of simply making people happy through food.

That's my north star.

To those just beginning their entrepreneurial path, I want to share a few lessons that have carried me through:

1. **Start with purpose** – If you're only chasing money, you'll burn out. But if you're chasing meaning, you'll find endurance.
2. **Outwork your fear** – Every entrepreneur has doubts. The key is to move anyway. Let your actions speak louder than your anxiety.
3. **Get comfortable being uncomfortable** – Growth lives outside the comfort zone. The moments that scare you most are often the ones that shape you most.
4. **Build your tribe** – Surround yourself with people who challenge, support, and inspire you. Energy is contagious; make sure it's positive.

5. **Keep learning** – Whether through books, mentors, or hard-earned experience, never stop sharpening your edge.
6. **Give back** – Success isn't success if you're the only one eating. Bring others to the table.
7. **Own your failures** – Mistakes don't define you; how you respond to them does.
8. **Celebrate the wins, but don't camp there** – Enjoy your victories, then get back to building.
9. **Stay human** – People do business with people, not logos. Let your personality, humility, and heart shine through.
10. **Never forget why you started** – Your origin story is your anchor. Let it keep you grounded when the waves hit.

Today, as I walk through Brasserie 19's dining room, greeting guests, checking in on dishes, and catching up with regulars, I don't feel tired; I feel alive. This isn't just a job, it's a calling. And it's far from over. I still have dreams to chase, people to mentor, and meals to create. The fire that started in a small Louisiana town is still burning strong.

My name is Charles Clark. I am a chef, a restaurateur, and an entrepreneur. And if there's one thing I've learned, it's this: Entrepreneurship is not about building a business. It's about building a life and making it worth remembering.

I have learned this, at least by my experiment: that IF one advances confidently towards the DIRECTION OF THEIR DREAMS and ENDEAVORS TO LIVE A LIFE which they IMAGINED, they will meet with success unexpected in common hours.

—Thoreau

KIMBERLY SHERER CUTCHALL

Kimberly Sherer Cutchall is a strategist, a truth-teller, and someone who cares deeply about helping people and organizations find their way forward. She has spent decades working with companies to simplify what feels complicated, align leaders around what matters, and prepare for whatever comes next. She does this with perspective, humor, and a belief that serious work does not require a serious ego.

Her work lives where business and humanity meet. Kimberly helps leaders understand themselves, their impact, and the ripple effects of their choices. She believes clarity creates confidence and that when people feel grounded in who they are, they lead with more intention and heart. Whether she is guiding a team through major transformation or coaching leaders to navigate complexity with confidence, her purpose is steady: help people see their potential and step toward it.

Kimberly is currently pursuing her PhD in International Business, with research focused on emotional intelligence and positive psychology. She speaks, writes, and consults with leaders around the world, offering insights that invite reflection, open new possibilities, and encourage meaningful action.

A lifelong learner, Kimberly believes we are all in progress and that life gets richer when we are honest about what we want and brave enough to grow. She is also the mother of Emerson and Mac, two strong and curious humans who keep her anchored to what matters most. They remind her daily that legacy is not about titles or achievements. It is about presence, connection, and how we show up for the people who trust us.

Kimberly@Cutchall.net

CHAPTER 7

YOU. ONLY BETTER.

by Kimberly Sherer Cutchall

Most people think leadership is about a title.
It's not.
Leadership is about influence -- and every one of us has it.
Whether you have the corner office or not, you impact the people and the spaces around you.
You set a tone. You create an atmosphere.
And that's where I want to start.

Most people move through their day like a thermometer.
They react to whatever's happening around them.
If the room is tense, they get tense.
If the mood is heavy, they get heavy.
They take the temperature… they don't set it.

But the best leaders?
They're like thermostats.
They don't just measure the mood -- they set the temperature.
They walk into a room and create clarity when there's confusion.
They bring calm when things are heated.
They lift the energy when people are drained.

And here's the truth:
You don't need a title to do that.
You don't need to change who you are.
You just need to understand who you are at your best -- and how to align yourself to that version more often.

That's **You. Only Better.**

Not a louder, flashier version of you.
Not a perfect version of you -- because let's be honest, perfection is the one thing at which you're guaranteed to fail. Every. Single. Time.
Excellence, however?
Excellence is alive. It evolves.
It's the art of constantly editing… your choices, your behaviors, your assumptions -- again and again, in both the big moments and the quiet ones.
Excellence is a lifelong pursuit, not a finish line.
It asks you to stay awake, stay aware, and stay in the work.
That's what makes it honest. That's what makes it sustainable.
That's what makes it human.
It's messy. It's humbling. It never ends.
And that's exactly what makes it powerful.
Because excellence makes space for growth. Perfection shuts it down.

This chapter is about that work.
About seeing yourself clearly.
About owning the ripple effects you create when you're at your best… and when you're not.
And about learning how to recalibrate, regulate, and return to your best, over and over again.
Because that's where your real leadership lives.
And make no mistake -- when you aren't intentional about this, you pay a price.

You pay it in the form of stressed teams, missed opportunities, and eroded trust.
But the most dangerous part?
You pay it in ways you can't always see.
People don't always tell you when they're shutting down.
They just stop bringing their best.
They start protecting themselves.
They disengage quietly.
And you? You keep charging ahead, unaware of the slow bleed happening behind you.
That's why self-awareness isn't a leadership luxury -- it's a leadership necessity.
Because ignoring your impact doesn't make it go away. It just makes it invisible to you… and painfully visible to everyone else.

Who Are You at Your Best?

Think about it.
Who are you at your best?
What does it look like when you're in flow -- when your strengths are properly aligned, your energy is contagious, and people lean in because they feel seen, heard, and inspired by you?

Maybe when you're at your best, you're a calm anchor in chaos.
Maybe you're the leader who lights a spark, makes people feel seen, or brings playful energy into the room.
Maybe you're the one who brings precision, structure, or boldness when it's needed most.
There's no one right way.
But there is a right you.
And if you can't name it, how will anyone else experience it?
That's why I challenge leaders to write it down, share it, and reflect on it often.

Because your best isn't static.
It evolves.
And your job is to evolve with it.

When you are at your best, the ripple effects are extraordinary.
You make better decisions.
You create space for others to contribute.
You unlock energy in your teams.
You drive progress without leaving people behind.
You become the leader people want to follow, not the one they have to follow.

But here's the problem: Most of us rarely pause to define what our best actually looks like.
We hope we'll recognize it when we feel it.
But that's not good enough for leaders today.
You have to name it.
You have to own it.
You have to practice it.

Who Are You at Your Worst?

And then comes the uncomfortable part.
You have to define who you are when you're not at your best.
Because we all have that version.
I call it your shadow self.
The version that shows up when you're triggered, overwhelmed, or protecting something.
For some, it's being sharp, curt, sarcastic.
For others, it's withdrawing, going silent, or over-controlling.
Whatever it is, you've got it.
And if you don't know what it is -- trust me, the people around you do.

And if you really want to see your shadow side -- ask the people who experience you the most.

Your team.
Your significant other.
Your kids.
They've seen it.
And I guarantee they could describe it in painful, accurate detail.
This isn't about self-criticism.
It's about radical honesty.
Because your shadow self is still you -- it's just you out of alignment.
It's you protecting, posturing, avoiding, or over-controlling.
And the sooner you can see it for what it is -- a default mode that kicks in under stress -- the sooner you can start to interrupt it.
Not because you're weak.
But because you're human.

Let me give you an example.
I once worked with a senior executive -- we'll call him Joe.
Joe was brilliant.
Sharp.
Decisive.
On paper, exactly what you'd want in a leader.
But Joe had a shadow side -- he didn't see it, but everyone around him did.
When things got tough, Joe doubled down on control.
He micromanaged.
He interrogated.
He became the loudest, most intense person in the room.
His intention?
To protect the team and organization from risk.
But the impact?
His team shut down.
They stopped speaking up.
They stopped offering solutions.
And eventually, they started leaving.

One by one.
When we worked together, Joe wasn't defensive about this; he was devastated.
Because once he finally saw it, he realized he had been leading from fear, not from his best self.
And his team?
They weren't afraid of failure.
They were afraid of him.
Joe's wake was bigger than he realized -- and it wasn't the one he wanted to leave behind.

When you are not at your best, your impact doesn't stay in your head.
It creates a turbulent wake.
It ripples out.
It creates collateral damage.
It erodes trust.
It silences voices.
It slows progress.
It creates a culture of fear, confusion, or disengagement.
I'm not telling you this to make you feel bad.
I'm telling you this to free you.

Because once you know what you look like at your best -- and at your worst -- you can start to catch yourself.
That's emotional intelligence in action.
That's the work of self-regulation.
That's the work of choosing, moment by moment, how you show up.

This is why I tell leaders: Your job isn't to be perfect.
It's to catch yourself faster.
To recover quicker.
To choose the better version of you sooner.
That's regulation in action.

And it's what separates leaders who exhaust themselves trying to hold it all together from leaders who stay grounded, connected, and clear-headed -- no matter what comes at them.
That's where leadership resilience is built.
Not in avoiding triggers, but in catching yourself mid-trigger and choosing differently.

The Ripple Effect of You

Let's make it real.

When you're at your best, what does that create?

- In people?
- In projects?
- In culture?

Write it down. Own it.

When I work with leaders, I ask them these simple, but profound, questions:

- **When I'm at my best, people feel…**
- **When I'm at my best, decisions are…**
- **When I'm at my best, teams move…**

And then the hard ones:

- **When I'm not at my best, people feel…**
- **When I'm not at my best, decisions get…**
- **When I'm not at my best, teams…**

This isn't about judgment.
It's about clarity.
When you can see the ripple effects of your behavior, you start to own your wake.

That wake can be smooth, giving people an easy path to follow -- or rough and choppy, making it hard for anyone to stay on course.
You realize leadership isn't about your intentions -- it's about the experience you create.
And that's what separates leaders who are tolerated from leaders who are trusted.

And make no mistake, the ripple of you doesn't just impact the next meeting or the next project.
It shapes the culture over time.
It shapes what people say about you when you leave the room -- or when you leave the organization altogether.
Because here's the thing, leaders often forget: your legacy isn't built in the big moments.
It's built in the small ones.
The hallway conversations.
The way you respond under pressure.
The tone you set when people bring you bad news.
Those are the moments people remember.
Those are the moments that either make people want to run toward you -- or around you.
And over time, that becomes your brand.
Not the speeches you give.
Not the emails you send.
The daily lived experience you create around you.
That's what people stay for… or leave to escape.

Here's the hard truth:
If you're not intentionally creating the experience you want others to have around you, you're still creating an experience -- it's just not the one you intended.
And people won't always tell you.
They'll adjust around you.

They'll adapt.
But inside, they'll be retreating.
And what could have been a thriving, collaborative culture becomes a transactional, check-the-box one.
That's the silent tax of leaders who never do this work.

The Work of Regulation

Most leaders assume emotional regulation is about staying calm all the time.
It's not.
It's about staying connected to the version of you that is most constructive and impactful -- even when the heat is on.
Sometimes that means turning down your intensity.
Sometimes it means dialing up your presence.
Sometimes it means pausing entirely before you act or speak.
This is what I call real-time leadership.
Not reacting.
Responding.
On purpose.

So, how do you regulate yourself in the heat of the moment?
How do you catch yourself when your strengths are out of alignment -- either too muted or too loud?

Here's what I coach leaders to practice:

1. **Catch it.**
    - You can't change what you can't see.
    - Build self-awareness practices into your day.
    - Ask people you trust to give you honest feedback.
    - Pay attention to your own cues -- your body, your tone, your behaviors.

2. **Name it.**
   - Label your state out loud -- especially when you're leading teams.
   - "I'm noticing I'm frustrated right now, and I don't want that to derail this conversation."
   - This is leadership gold. It disarms the room and models emotional intelligence in action.

3. **Choose it.**
   - Ask yourself:
   - "Is this the version of me I want leading this conversation?"
   - "What would my best self do right now?"
   - Leadership is a choice.
   - And the pause to choose is where power lives.

4. **Practice it.**
   - Emotional regulation is a practice.
   - It's not a switch you flip once and it's done.
   - Build rituals into your day that reset you.
   - Reflection. Breathwork. Movement.
   - Whatever works for you -- but do it on purpose.

5. **Repair it.**
   - When you get it wrong (and you will), own it.
   - Go back to the team. Name the moment. Apologize if needed.
   - Trust isn't built on perfection -- it's built on repair.

In fact, some of the most powerful leadership moments I've ever witnessed weren't when leaders got it right the first time.

It was when they got it wrong -- and then came back to the team and said, "I missed it. I didn't handle that well. Let's reset."

That's where teams lean in.

That's where psychological safety is built.
Not through flawless execution, but through visible ownership.
Because when you do that, you model something even more powerful than expertise... You model what it looks like to be human and own your space.
And that's a leadership move that creates permission for others to do the same.

Here's where most leaders miss the mark -- they think if they admit they were off, they'll lose credibility.
In reality, the opposite is true.
When you circle back, own the moment, and repair the relationship -- you build trust.
People don't expect perfection from you.
They expect humanity.
They expect honesty.
They expect you to own your moments.
That's what makes you credible, relatable, and worth following.

This Is the Work

So let me ask you:

- Where in your leadership are you reacting out of habit instead of choosing with intention?
- What situations or patterns consistently pull you into your shadow self -- and what's the cost to you and those around you when you stay there?
- If you paused in those moments and chose to show up as the best version of you, how might your impact -- and your leadership legacy -- change?

These aren't questions to journal once and move on from.
They're questions to keep on your desk.

On your phone.
In your conversations with people who will tell you the truth.
Because leadership isn't a one-and-done activity.
It's a daily practice.
And the leaders who commit to this kind of daily awareness?
They build teams who trust faster.
Cultures that move faster.
And organizations that withstand pressure without falling apart.

Leadership is a privilege.
And with that privilege comes the responsibility to own your impact.
To see yourself clearly.
To own the version of you that lifts others -- and the version that might hold them back.
To practice. To regulate. To choose.
It's not easy work.
It's messy.
It's unglamorous.
It's the kind of work that rarely gets a trophy… but it's the work that makes the difference.
Because titles fade.
Positional power shifts.
But the way you made people feel… that sticks.
That becomes your leadership legacy.
That becomes your brand.
And that's not built by accident.
It's built by the daily, disciplined choice to show up as You. Only Better.
Over and over again.
On purpose.

You. Only Better.

Not someone else.
Not an over-engineered, always-on, untouchable leader.
But you… fully owned, fully accountable, fully human.
That's the kind of leader the world is desperate for right now.

So the question isn't:

- Can you become someone better?

The real question is:

- Are you willing to own the best version of who you already are… and choose to show up as that version… on purpose?

That's your work.

That's the work of **You. Only Better.**

KAREN DEGEURIN

Karen Remington is the President and Co-Founder of Remington Insurance Brokers, where she leads with heart, experience, and a lifelong commitment to helping others. With more than 30 years of service in human resources, health care, and insurance, Karen has built a reputation for combining strategic leadership with genuine compassion. Before launching her own firm, she served as an Executive Sales Leader with HealthMarkets and an Agent Manager with UnitedHealthcare, following a distinguished career in human resources with Continental Airlines, Arthur Andersen, and Waste Management.

A proud Houston native and graduate of the University of Texas, Karen co-founded Remington Insurance Brokers in 2020 and has since grown the company into a thriving network of agents serving clients across the country.

Deeply dedicated to her community, Karen has spent nearly three decades volunteering with the Houston Livestock Show and Rodeo, earning the Chairman's Award for her leadership. She has also chaired and supported events for Kids' Meals, Dec My Room, American Cancer Society, Today's Harbor for Children, and many others.

Recognized for her service and leadership, Karen was named a 2026 Woman of Distinction Houston, honoring her passion for people, purpose, and community impact.

RemingtonBrokers.com

"You don't have to do it alone."

CHAPTER 8

THE BEGINNING: FROM RELUCTANT SALESPERSON TO PASSIONATE PROFESSIONAL

By Karen DeGeurin

I didn't grow up dreaming of a career in insurance. In fact, my first job or my first stab at being an entrepreneur was being a cheerleader coach for young girls. I was picked from a group of nationally ranked cheerleaders to train young cheerleaders, and then I was part of a small group of people that hosted the first nationally televised cheerleading championships, where the winners were awarded scholarships to college. I then began the first "Cheerleading Gym", teaching girls not associated with a school cheerleading squad, and took them to the national cheerleading championships. My teams placed or won the championships, and many of the girls were awarded a scholarship to college. I traveled around the United States coaching girls and teams, getting them ready for competition, hired by their parents, hoping that their child would win a scholarship. What a great start to my entrepreneurial life. However, imagine this: in my late twenties, I felt like I had aged out of cheerleading and took my undergrad and graduate degrees from the University of Texas, and went to work at Continental Airlines in the Human Resources department.

My life at Continental was during the "worst to first" years under the direction of Gordon Bethune. I learned how to standardize human resources and payroll systems due to all Continental's mergers and acquisitions. Additionally, being part of the cultural merge of newly acquired employees gave me an education that is equivalent to a PHD. This education opened the doors for me to become a consultant with Arthur Anderson. Flying around America, meeting with blue-chip clients, developing and delivering talent acquisition, compensation, benefits, and company program and support systems. But I wanted to help people one on one. I was working in a different field altogether, and someone suggested I try my hand at Medicare sales. At the time, I thought, "Insurance? Isn't that dry and complicated?" Then, I thought of it as a possible side hustle.

Turns out, it is complicated. But it's also deeply important. I took the steps to become licensed, contracted and certified and went to work.

I remember my first few appointments vividly. Sitting at kitchen tables, talking to folks who were confused about Medicare. They had questions that no one was answering. They feared making a wrong move. And I realized something: this was more than a job. This was a chance to *protect people's dignity* during one of the most vulnerable transitions of their lives, turning 65.

That realization lit a fire within me. I studied the products. I asked questions. I attended every training I could find. I shadowed successful agents and built processes that worked. Eventually, I built a book of business that not only sustained me but gave me the confidence to grow beyond just "me."

I launched my first insurance brokerage agency 18 years ago. I was living my dream of having my own company established clients, marketing my business, and had contracts with the top ten carriers in America. Then one of those carriers, United HealthCare, came knocking and asked me to be the agent manager in Houston, Texas. I was back in corporate America, and it felt good… for a while

The Power of Leadership: Building a Team with Intention

Sales success opened the door to leadership. But being a great agent doesn't automatically make you a great leader and it was time to grow again.

When I was asked to help recruit and develop agents for Empower Brokerage's Houston office, I saw it as more than a title; it was a responsibility. These were real people trusting me with their careers. And I knew what was at stake. Most agents entering this industry aren't prepared. They're overwhelmed by compliance, confused about commissions, and unsure where to find clients.

So, I set out to build an office that didn't just look good on paper; it worked. We opened our training space, built a compliance-first culture, and developed an onboarding process that simplified the complex. I didn't want to just hire agents; I wanted to *launch careers.*

Our office became a hub. We held Medicare boot camps, hosted carrier expos, and ran community education events. We made it a point to train, mentor, and support agents like they were family. Because in a business that can feel isolating, *culture* is everything.

And it worked. We didn't just grow in size. We grew in strength.

Stepping Back into Ownership: The Birth of Remington Insurance Brokers

In 2022, after years of building teams and leading under someone else's brand, I knew it was time to take the leap. Alongside my husband and business partner Peter Remington, we launched **Remington Insurance Brokers**.

It wasn't just about putting our name on the door; it was about building something that reflected our values. We wanted a company that stood for possibility, purpose, and professionalism. A place where agents could thrive, clients could be confident, and the community could count on us.

From day one, we set out to do things differently.

- We **trained agents in real-world scenarios**, not just PowerPoint presentations.
- We **invested in marketing tools and compliant funnels**, so our agents weren't out there cold-calling.
- We **created a coaching environment** where mentorship wasn't optional; it was built into the culture.
- And we **focused on Medicare, life, dental, and group health benefits**, so we could offer holistic, needs-based planning.

Our growth has been exciting, but what I'm most proud of is the reputation we've built. We're not the biggest firm in Texas, but we are one of the most respected. And that's because we never compromise on integrity.

Mentorship: The Multiplication of Impact

One of the greatest honors of my career has been mentoring new agents, especially women entering this business later in life. I meet agents who are 55 years old, changing careers, scared of technology, and unsure if they can make it.

I always tell them: ***You absolutely can.***

You don't have to be young, tech-savvy, or aggressive to succeed in insurance. You must care. You must show up. You must do what you say you're going to do. That's it.

I mentor with realism. I don't sugarcoat how hard this can be. But I also mentor with optimism. I've seen agents go from zero to six figures in a year just by following the system, being coachable, and sticking with it.

Mentorship matters because this business can be lonely. When you're out in the field, navigating appointment cancellations or rejections, you need someone to call. Someone to say, "Hey, I've been there. Here's how I got through it."

I'm proud to be that voice for many agents. And I hope they'll be that voice for someone else one day.

What I've Learned as an Entrepreneur

Building a business from scratch, especially as a woman in a male-dominated industry, taught me a few key truths. If you're thinking of launching something of your own, take these to heart:

1. **Your name is your currency.**

    Reputation matters more than revenue. I'd rather walk away from a deal than compromise on ethics. Because in the long run, trust compounds.

2. **You can't build alone.**

    Success is a team sport. Surround yourself with people who believe in the mission and complement your weaknesses. And then lead them with humility.

3. **Don't wait to be "ready."**

    There's never a perfect time to launch, grow, or pivot. If you feel the nudge, take the step. Figure it out as you go. That's what entrepreneurs do.

4. **Lead with service.**

    Whether you're working with clients or agents, ask: "How can I help them win?" When you help others win, you build a business that lasts.

5. **Systems equal freedom.**

   The better your systems, the less you'll micromanage. Train well. Document everything. Automate what you can. Then focus on relationships.

6. **Stay coachable.**

   I'm still learning. I listen to podcasts, read industry news, and surround myself with peers who challenge me. Growth doesn't end; it evolves.

7. **Celebrate the wins.**

   Entrepreneurship is hard. Take time to reflect, recharge, and recognize progress. It's easy to focus only on what's next, but joy is found in what's now.

The Power of Purpose

The older I get, the more I realize that entrepreneurship isn't about building a business. It's about building a life that reflects your values.

For me, those values are:

- **Faith** – I believe this work is a calling. Helping people navigate Medicare, understand life insurance, and prepare for retirement is a ministry of service.
- **Family** – Working with my husband and my mother has been one of the greatest blessings of this journey. We complement each other's strengths and share a vision that keeps us grounded.
- **Freedom** – I've built a career that gives me time with loved ones, flexibility to travel, and the freedom to support causes I care about.
- **Fulfillment** – Watching agents I mentored buy their first home, earn awards, or take their kids on vacation because of this business, that's what fills my heart.

Legacy Leadership

Now that we've established Remington Insurance Brokers as a brand people trust, my role is shifting again. I'm thinking more about legacy. About how we replicate leadership. About how we create a business that thrives long after we're gone.

That's why we're investing in next-generation tools like CRM systems, compliant ad funnels, and digital learning platforms. That's why we're grooming new leaders inside our agency to step up and step in. That's why we're documenting our playbook and making our coaching scalable.

Because the future of this business isn't just mine, it belongs to every agent who believes in the mission.

Final Thoughts: For the Woman (or Man) on the Fence

If you're reading this and wondering if you have what it takes to become an entrepreneur, let me tell you: *you do.*

You don't need to be the loudest voice in the room. You don't need to know everything about insurance. You don't need a degree in finance or a perfect résumé.

What you need is the courage to begin. The humility to learn. The persistence to stay with it when it gets tough. And the heart to serve others with excellence.

That's how I built my business. That's how I lead my team. And that's how you'll change your life.

Because entrepreneurship isn't just about building income, it's about building impact.

And I'm here to tell you: *if I can do it, and if you have the same mindset, so can you.*

ADRIAN DUEÑAS

Adrian Dueñas is the founder and CEO of **BeDESIGN**, Houston's premier luxury furniture showroom celebrated for its exclusive European collections and visionary collaborations with world-renowned design brands. Born in Ecuador and raised internationally, Dueñas brings a global perspective to everything he creates, blending aesthetics, strategy, and cultural insight to shape the future of modern design.

After moving to Houston, he recognized the city's emerging potential as a design destination and, in 2016, co-founded BeDESIGN in Montrose with acclaimed interior designer Marcelo Saénz. The showroom quickly became a centerpiece of Houston's design community, known for representing elite brands such as Molteni&C, Paola Lenti, Flexform, B&B Italia, Maxalto, Ligne Roset, Poltona Frau, and Giorgetti. Under the umbrella of his Madrid-based firm, **Welcome Design**, Dueñas also oversees commercial and hospitality projects across Europe and North America.

Before BeDESIGN, he co-founded **Promostock**, a South American promotional products company serving global clients including Nestlé and Unilever.

A passionate supporter of the arts and philanthropy, Dueñas has chaired major cultural events and served on multiple nonprofit boards. Named **Ambassador of The Allen and Thompson Hotel** and **Brand Ambassador for Park House Houston**, he continues to champion design, culture, and community on a global scale.

> "Life has a way of getting better, even when facing the greatest obstacles. Trust yourself, work relentlessly, and remember that your network built on honest relationships will become your most valuable asset—one that no amount of money can buy."

adrianduenas.com
Be-design.us

Instagram
@adrianduenasm
@bedesign_official

CHAPTER 9

THE DESIGN OF A LIFE: MY ENTREPRENEURIAL BLUEPRINT

By Adrian Dueñas

As my therapist says, tell that kid in elementary or high school, "All will be better." And you know what? That is true. To that boy: look at me, look at all of us now. Cool, right? All will be awesome. But wait… let's go back a little bit in time. I was born and partially raised in Ecuador, a country where you either have a lot, pretend a lot, or have nothing. I had a very intellectual father from a mixed European family, and a high-class mom who taught me how to be good, go to church, and spoiled me like no other. My family was overprotective, with issues like any other. I was educated in an all-boys Catholic private school until junior year, when I begged to be moved; that wasn't easy. I jumped from school to school until I finally graduated from high school in Northern California. I initially tried to stay in California for college, but then I moved to New York. Around age 22 or 23, while visiting family in Ecuador, I met the love of my life, and yes, it was the love of my life. I decided to drop out of college in the U.S. and finish back in Ecuador.

During that transition, my dad passed away after a long battle with cancer, and this is where my entrepreneurial path begins. The family was stressed and disrupted. I had found love and was finishing college. I knew I had to survive somehow. When the head of the family passes, you learn a lot about finances, shortages, and sudden disruptions that are not as easy as you expected. In my last year of college, I asked my brother to join me in opening a business, where I would handle the management, and he would maintain his current job. He put up the money. I also asked Marcelo, my then (and now) life partner, for some more. And yes, one of the biggest promotional item companies in South America was born: Promostock.

As soon as I could, I learned how to apply for a business loan. I bought trucks to move the product that big companies started to buy. Then, a new telephone company came to Ecuador in 2002, Alegro PCS. This small country suddenly had a huge new cellphone company. I had an assistant, a fax machine, and a long list of promotional items to quote. Yes, Gen Z, we used faxes back in the day! But I only had it for a year or so, then email came. I'm not that old! The quote request was an insane amount, one we'd dream of selling in an entire year. 100,000 T-shirts. 50,000 baseball caps. On and on. I became friends with the girls who worked at the marketing agency, Young & Rubicam. No entertainment budget for me or anyone, just smiles, jokes, charm, fast info sent by fax or in person, samples, and a small hope of getting at least 10% of the order. One day, I arrived at my office, and my assistant said, "Look on your desk. There's a fax directed to you." Yes, it was the entire order, sent to my tiny new company. I couldn't believe it. I reread the numbers maybe ten times. I added, subtracted, multiplied, and yes, that was it. My jackpot. And then… experience (or lack of it) kicked in. I needed a warranty to get this big advance to start production. No credit history. No dad to ask for help. I asked the agency if I could give them a check instead of using insurance, as it was too expensive and would increase the price. (You now understand that wasn't the only issue.) The finance director, a woman with a clean haircut, thick glasses, and a serious look, stared at me. "Oh, you're the guy who's always laughing with our account directors," she said. I smiled: "Yes, that sure is me. I'm very funny." She immediately burst out laughing and broke character. She said, "We never do this, but I'll do it for you. I need your check and a promissory note." Guess what, I didn't have a personal checkbook. Nor did I know what a promissory note was. Just checks from the company. I replied with no hesitation: "Sure, no problem. Let me go get it." I asked Marcelo for a blank check. Hey, we'd only been dating for two years or less. I must've been really good to get his trust.

Well… after that, I kept managing the business for more than 12 years. It grew so much that I traveled to China multiple times, Europe, the U.S., and became the main supplier for Nestlé and Unilever across South America and Mexico. Later, I sold my shares to my brother. They're now the in-house buyers for Unilever, one of the biggest food and home product companies. Many challenges happened over those years, but here we are. The company is still profitable and open. Along the way, we opened different companies to support the big one textile production, a small Shanghai office, printing facilities, and more.

Meanwhile, my fascination with Marcelo's interior design work kept growing. I was part of many projects. Security issues in Ecuador made us think about moving. But where? When? How? Our mutual love for Madrid and my obsession with the U.S., especially New York, were always on the table. Life back home was very comfortable, with lots of services and support. But our best friend Karen had moved to Houston. We visited her often. Other friends from Dubai were also moving there. A tiny spark began. We hired a company in New York for a business plan, fingers crossed, and dreaming of Miami, NY, even LA, or San Francisco.

Marcelo had been doing interior design since the day we met, yes, the Marcelo Saenz of Marcelo Saenz & Associates. We met a good friend who owned a European furniture shop. He was a great client, and we thought, "Let's replicate this in the U.S. "

What started as a partnership eventually turned into just us. The multi-line concept became ultra-luxury: Italian, French, and Spanish interior brands. A 5,000 sq ft boutique in the heart of Houston. Well… Houston can be tricky when it comes to finding a lease location that matches your ambition. After almost a year of looking at crazy dates, awful spaces, and overpriced strip malls, we did the math and decided to buy a lot and build.

Yes, like that. While still under a business visa. I met a friend in Madrid who introduced me to the CEO of BBVA, a Spanish bank operating in the U.S. We put down 30%, financed the lot, and used private equity to build. In the middle of it, we had to ask for more money. We had the most stressful two years of building. New country. New city. Rules and requirements we didn't even know existed. A surprise full-sized elevator? Of course. We finally opened the doors of BeDESIGN on January 4, 2016, but the company had been open since 2013.

During those two pre-opening years, we invented every possible way to keep things going. And here's the biggest piece of advice I can give: We used those two years to network. We met the weirdest artists and the wealthiest people in town. We learned about the art scene, the nonprofit circuit, and the gala calendar. We fell in love with the Menil and made friends at the Museum of Fine Arts. This gave our brand a reputation and gave us real cultural weight in the city. Four years later, I was getting my back cracked by our next-door neighbor, a well-known chiropractor. I mentioned we needed more space. He said he needed more parking. I asked, "Would you sell the lot?" He said yes. And just like that, a real estate deal was closed while my bones were popping. We bought it, unified the two lots, and built a three-story showroom over

20,000 sq ft of European design, with a rooftop that looks like spring in Italy or a lounge from the Monaco Yacht Show. And yes, we had to trash the first building's elevator and buy a new one.

There's never enough experience when construction is involved. We also learned that real estate is king. We bought other properties, beautified them, and made a good profit. We invested in new high-rises, which made us visible and brought in even more business. We partnered with the best. Parallel to that, I started my own brand, working with well-known American designers to license their products to top European brands.

I've also built a personal brand and network that connects businesses and individuals to align new income: from investments to private equity to partnerships. I found a strategy that doesn't make me the biggest part of the business or the smallest. It makes me the middleman. And you know what? Being the middleman is the best. You're the glue. The bone structure. And if you sell yourself well with a strong moral compass, honesty, and responsibility, things flow. Remember: selling is everything. Doctors, lawyers, gardeners, carpenters, presidents, we all sell every day. I use my best skill, which is no secret: humor, charm, and relatability. I'm here, and I'm not going anywhere, even if some competitors would pay good money for what I've built. This network and opportunity started early in my career. The only difference now is that it's profitable. People don't just get my time; they get a business commitment.

It's not just nice. It's necessary.

And it's taken me places. I've been an ambassador for banks, foundations, hotels, and developments. I've planned Oscar parties with Elton John and his AIDS Foundation (Are we really here?). I've represented the iconic Cornelia Street home in New York (yes, the Taylor Swift one!). I've found partners who became family, like my best friend Nina Magon. With her, I've traveled the world. We've cried on each other's shoulders, watched people come and go, and always found new business opportunities. Together, we launched her book with an exclusive Balmain collaboration.

We styled the Mandarin Oriental penthouse in LA with a fashion show. We launched the book again during Dubai Design Week.

What–A–Journey.

As I wrap up this chapter, I'm flying back from San Juan, Puerto Rico, after touring a magnificent new development. I'll head home, pack, and leave for Los Cabos to finish a dream project in Chileno Bay.

Yes, I'm name-dropping and bragging while I sip a glass of wine. But I earned it, and I want to end the same way I began. To that 15-year-old boy. To the 22-year-old who lost his dad and had no idea where life would go. Look at us. We're tan, sipping wine, jumping from project to project. We're fine. More than fine.

To anyone reading this, whether you're young, just starting, or starting again: All gets better.

Cheers to hard work and dreams that come true.

There is no plan "B"
If you have a Plan B, then you're expecting Plan A to fail.
You may have to pivot to achieve Plan A, but it's always your goal.
Edison had to pivot thousands of times before he
created the light bulb.

TOD EASON

William Tod Eason is a Houston-based entrepreneur, investor, and financial strategist whose career spans multiple industries, including wealth management, venture capital, energy, media, and emerging technologies.

Born in 1970 at Reese Air Force Base in Lubbock, Texas, Eason grew up in a military family and spent his early years moving between Washington, Colorado, and ultimately Boerne, Texas. He graduated from Texas A&M University in 1993 with a degree in psychology and began his career in real estate development and corporate management before joining American Express in Shreveport, Louisiana, as a wealth manager. There, he helped launch a new credit union branch and began developing early ventures in timber, oil, and gas.

Eason went on to found an independent wealth management firm in Chicago and later relocated to Houston, where he has since advised and invested in projects across industries, from healthcare and film finance to digital media and artificial intelligence. He was a co-founder and managing partner of CultureMap.com, a leading digital lifestyle platform, and more recently co-founded an AI company focused on enabling small businesses to compete for government contracts.

As a guest author in this collaborative volume, Eason draws on decades of real-world experience navigating volatile markets, scaling startups, and aligning capital with opportunity. His contribution offers readers a grounded, candid perspective on entrepreneurship, risk, and the long game of building value across industries.

> "You earn the right to solve more complex problems"
> –*Tod Eason*

CHAPTER 10

FROM MARKETS TO MEDIA: MY JOURNEY THROUGH ENTREPRENEURSHIP, MENTORSHIP, AND CHAOS

By Tod Eason

If someone asked me to describe my career in one word, I'd say eclectic, which is a polite way of saying I have the professional attention span of a golden retriever in a squirrel sanctuary. Call it curiosity or adult-onset ADHD, but it's led to a weirdly satisfying journey through digital media, commercial real estate, investment banking, and more startup experiments than Lady Gaga has changed costumes. The common thread? Entrepreneurship. That, and a stubborn belief that if you keep learning (and occasionally falling on your face), you'll eventually figure something out or at least have a decent dinner party story. Just as rewarding as building businesses has been mentoring others trying to carve their own strange and exciting paths, usually while convincing them that yes, the panic they're feeling is completely normal.

Early Signs and Big Leaps

My entrepreneurial "spark" started early, meaning I was hustling other kids out of their lunch money long before I needed to shave. I flipped free radio station stickers for quarters in elementary school and somehow convinced people that cinnamon-flavored toothpicks were worth a buck. Honestly, I might've peaked in fifth grade. From there, it was lawn mowing, dog walking, basically any job that paid in real money or baseball cards. By high school, I was deep into stock investing while most of my peers were focused on homecoming dates and getting their learner's permits. I was reading annual reports like bedtime stories. It took a while for that to catch on with the ladies.

At Texas A&M, I studied psychology partly because I was curious about what made people tick, and partly because I figured understanding the human mind might help explain my obsession with business plans written on napkins. After college, I went into financial services and eventually launched my own firm. Managing money for other people teaches you two important things very quickly:

- Trust is everything.
- You're not as smart as you think you are, so you'd better keep learning.

I'm proud of the work I did in that chapter of my life. I helped real people make meaningful changes. And when you manage someone's life savings, you learn fast that you're essentially on emergency speed dial somewhere between priest and therapist.

From Finance to Media (Wait, What?)

I've never been great at sticking to one lane. My brain runs like a web browser with 37 tabs open at all times. So, naturally, I left finance to co-found a digital media company. Makes perfect sense, right? In 2008, I walked into a meeting to talk about a restaurant deal and walked out co-founding CultureMap with the inimitable Lonnie Schiller. We never even got to the restaurant pitch. Somewhere between his idea about a new kind of local content and my inability to leave a whiteboard untouched, we had a startup.

We launched in Houston, then expanded across Texas with one simple goal: help people connect with their city in a way that didn't feel like eating dry toast. Somehow, it worked. We grew to about $3 million in revenue and exited in 2015. It taught me how to build something people actually care about, how to become a good business partner, and that when you're surrounded by great people, sometimes the best business plans begin with forgetting why you walked into the room in the first place. Oh, and during that time, with my good buddy John Rentz, I helped structure the financing of a little indie film called Crazy Heart. It ended up winning an Oscar or two. No big deal. I mean, I mostly contributed spreadsheets, snacks, and sarcasm, but I'll still mention it at parties like I was personally responsible for Jeff Bridges' performance.

Building and Bridging Worlds

After CultureMap, I hit reset. I took some time off. Got divorced. I went to Europe. Played full-time dad. Not necessarily in that order, and sometimes all in the same week. I didn't miss a single playdate or school festival. "Dad" is still the best job title I've ever had, even though it pays in Legos and the feedback is mostly "My ponytail is too tight!"

Eventually, it was time to make money again. I considered launching a stripped-down version of CultureMap just for middle-aged men, possibly called DadMap (tagline: Know Where the Clean Bathrooms Are). I even started a book on divorce (still in the "therapeutic journaling with delusions of grandeur" phase). Instead, I pivoted into consulting for a very specific reason.

That consulting journey led me everywhere from consumer food events to overseeing distressed asset valuations in Canada. Because when you're in transition, there's nothing more comforting than flying to the frozen oilfields and trying to appraise broken things.

Apparently, I developed a reputation for being the guy to call when a project was on fire. Not in a fun, "bring marshmallows" way. More like, "this business might not survive next week, please help" kind of way. I became a fixer, a problem-solver, and sometimes a professional bad-news translator. It was scary, rewarding, and occasionally made me question every career choice I'd ever made, but it taught me this: you earn the right to solve more complex problems by being willing to climb into the trenches.

The Latest Adventures: Real Estate, Tech, and Scary AI

A few years ago, I had the opportunity to work with Paul Coonrod, a sharp, forward-thinking entrepreneur I've known for years, as he navigated early-stage AI tech while building Pagewood, a commercial real estate investment firm centered on people and powered by a tech-driven vision. Speaking of AI, I've also been involved in building some incredibly inventive tech that connects businesses with government contracts, especially within the Department of Defense. That company secured several government grants of its own and continues to navigate the, let's say…dynamic world of federal agencies where the rules, priorities, and acronyms seem to change weekly. Scratch that daily. Okay, fine: hourly. High school civics definitely didn't prepare us for this version of government. I've also kept a toe in the startup world through investment banking relationships, working with early-stage founders in sectors like AI, defense, and consumer products. These days, I split my time between advisory roles, part-time C-level gigs, and full-time startup therapist, cheering founders on as they try to turn chaos into traction. I'm also knee-deep in learning how plaintiff law firms operate, something I definitely didn't see coming. But here we go. Staying curious has kept me relevant. The moment you rely too heavily on what you used to know, you officially become that guy telling Gen Z about dial-up internet. (Which I also do, at every opportunity.)

The Real ROI: Mentorship

As fun as building businesses can be, helping other people build theirs is even better. Over the years, I've mentored dozens of founders, investors, and professionals. Some have raised millions. Others changed careers entirely. And some just needed someone to say, "No, you're not crazy, this is hard."

I've been incredibly lucky with my own mentors. They've been wise, hilarious, honest, and usually better dressed. Knowing who to call when you're stuck is one of the most valuable life skills you can build. It starts with listening. It ends with listening more. (Bonus points if you buy the first round.)

My mentorship style? I ask questions. Usually, the same ones someone once asked me:

- What do you actually want?
- What's getting in the way?
- What are you willing to risk?

Spoiler alert: I rarely have the answers. But I'm pretty good at holding up a mirror and helping people see what's already there, minus the self-doubt and bad lighting.

Lessons Learned (Mostly the Hard Way)

Some things you learn from mentors. Others you learn from screwing up repeatedly and hoping nobody noticed. Here are a few of mine:

- You can't outwork a bad strategy. You can burn through all your energy and capital trying, though. Ask me how I know.

- Culture = Everything. Work with good people. Life's too short to suffer through meetings with people who make your ears want to commit suicide.
- You'll never feel ready. But if something both excites and terrifies you, that's probably your brain signaling: Hey, maybe we're onto something.
- Success is seasonal. Sometimes you grind. Sometimes you rest. And sometimes you just stare at your operating account and hit refresh until the wire hits, then contemplate moving to a cabin with no Wi-Fi.

Giving Back to Houston. Houston has been my home for 23 years. It's gritty, diverse, underestimated, and endlessly surprising, basically everything I aspire to be, minus the humidity. I've tried to pour back into this city through boards, events, and mentoring. I've supported local artists, coached startup founders, and helped people shape their stories, their strategies, and occasionally their pitch decks. The truth is that cities don't thrive because of infrastructure or policy; they thrive because of people. And Houston has some of the best damn people I know.

What's Next?

For me, "next" usually lands somewhere between a calculated decision and a happy accident, part strategy, part blindfolded leap. Right now, I'm in a bit of a transition phase (again), keeping my eyes open and my calendar just open enough for something unexpected to walk in.

Lately, I've been poking around in agri-business, lifestyle brands, and ideas that could make travel more meaningful or at least less annoying. I'm also intrigued by how we can build smart, thoughtful products for my parents' generation, the folks with most of the wisdom and, not coincidentally, most of the money. I've been thinking a lot about what it means to stay useful without becoming a relic. That means saying yes more often than no. It means surrounding yourself with interesting people from wildly different paths. It means buying a stranger a drink, even if they talk too much about crypto or CrossFit.

Also, I've been toying with the idea of putting together a deal to buy the Pittsburgh Pirates. They clearly need help. But it also feels like a trap. Still a Cubs fan. Life is complicated.

So, here's my (solicited) closing advice because someone asked me to write this and I try to be helpful:

- Stay curious.
- Be generous with your time and your attention.
- Say yes to the random coffee meeting, you never know what rabbit hole it might lead you down.
- And every now and then, let yourself "waste" time. That's often where the best stuff is hiding.

As for what's next? I don't know. But I'll probably sketch it out on a napkin.

GRETCHEN GILLIAM

Gretchen Gilliam is a proud lifelong Texan whose entrepreneurial spirit is matched only by her love for adventure—whether she is closing real estate deals or riding horses on her ranch in Fulshear. A graduate of the **University of Texas at Austin** with a B.B.A. in marketing, Gilliam built a successful career in real estate as president of **Gilliam Properties Management Company**, where she brokered retail and commercial development projects throughout Texas.

In her midfifties, Gilliam fulfilled a lifelong dream by transforming a motor home into the **Glamour Gypsies** mobile boutique. After two years on the road, she co-created **The Hive: A Pop-Up Collective**, and since 2023 has served as the sole owner of **The Hive** in Houston's Rice Village—a creative space supporting local artists, makers, and entrepreneurs.

Dedicated to community service, Gilliam has volunteered with the **Houston Livestock Show and Rodeo** for nearly forty years, serving on its board of directors and numerous committees, including Education Contributions, International, and Trailblazers. She is also a board member and former gala chair for **Amigas Para Niños**, mentoring young scholars and supporting children's initiatives across Texas.

Gilliam lives in Fulshear with her partner, entrepreneur **George Lane**, where life on the ranch continues to keep her grounded and inspired.

TheHivePopUp.com
@thehivepopup
@gretchen_gilliam_the_hive

CHAPTER 11

A COMMUNITY BUILT ON BEES

By Gretchen Gilliam

The Hive's name is more than clever branding. It's a symbol. A beehive thrives only when each bee does its job. It's a collective, not a solo act. In many ways, I created a retail model that mirrors that philosophy - every Showroom Partner plays a role, every product has a place, and every customer becomes part of the experience.

> **"Anyone who thinks they're too small to make a difference has never met the honey bee."** –Anonymous.

That quote has always resonated with me. Small acts, small ideas, small steps - when done with purpose - can lead to extraordinary results. I didn't start The Hive with millions of dollars or a team of consultants. I started it with a dream, some grit, a repurposed motor home, and a desire to create something different. Something meaningful.

Reinvention on Wheels – My Journey from Dream to Destination

Entrepreneurship is rarely a straight road. It curves through reinvention, bumps into failure, weaves through self-discovery, and, if you're lucky, arrives somewhere uniquely yours. For me, the journey began not with a detailed business plan, but with a childhood dream of having my own retail store and the courage to start over in my mid-50s. My story stands as a testament to the strength of starting from where you are, using what you have, and trusting yourself enough to leap, even later in life.

A Seed Planted in Youth

For as long as I could remember, I dreamed of going to the market, buying clothes, and opening a boutique space that felt welcoming, colorful, and fun. A place where fashion wasn't just sold but shared, where people didn't just shop but connected. When I began my studies at the University of Texas, I initially pursued a major in Textiles and Apparel. But just a week in, practicality pulled me toward a Business Marketing degree, something that, in time, would become a crucial asset. The knowledge I gained about branding, consumer behavior, and business strategy became a powerful asset.

While my career in commercial real estate would span over three decades, the boutique owner's dream never left. Instead, it incubated quietly in the background of managing tenants, negotiating leases, and handling budgets. My creative spark was saved for use in my volunteer endeavors, such as creating new initiatives for charities and planning galas.

Reinvention in Reverse

In my mid-50s, I found myself in a position to be able to revisit my dream of having my own store. The answer was literally in our backyard! We had an old motorhome sitting in our driveway that we rarely used. For months, I looked at it with this absurd idea of somehow turning it into a mobile boutique. This was really before fashion trucks were a "thing," and the few people I mentioned my idea to either thought I was crazy or just didn't understand the concept. Honestly, taking an older but perfectly good RV and totally gutting it scared me!

But I saw the success of food trucks, and the idea of a flexible schedule appealed to me. I leaned into my decades of business experience and decided to "go for it". When I wasn't learning everything I could about the retail clothing business, I spent hours in the motorhome visualizing the layout – where to hang the clothes, store inventory, set up the checkout stand, etc. I found a contractor who decided to work with me (I think he thought I was a little crazy, too), but he was up to the challenge and created a beautiful boutique-on-wheels.

While the renovation was taking place, I flew out to the Los Angeles Market on my first buying trip. After years of thinking about this moment, I quickly realized nothing prepares you for hands-on experience. I had taken a bold leap, but that didn't mean I had it all figured out. This first buying trip was a humbling wake-up call. Despite my business experience, I was new to the fashion retail industry. But instead of faking confidence, I leaned into vulnerability. I asked questions. I admitted what I didn't know, and I discovered that people in the industry were more than willing to help, because honesty invites support, and humility earns trust. And I found that vulnerability invites support in ways pride never can. By late 2017, the Glamour Gypsies fashion truck was on the road, rolling up to festivals, markets, and pop-ups around Houston and beyond.

From Fashion Truck to Brick and Mortar

Those two years in the truck were a crash course in retail. I learned how to merchandise in tight spaces, adapt inventory for different crowds, and connect quickly with customers in temporary settings. It provided me with real-time feedback and the confidence to take the next step. Eventually, I joined a shared retail space, like what this book represents. It was a community of small business owners working together under one roof. It was collaborative, affordable, and a perfect stepping stone.

Then the unexpected happened: our landlord lost the lease, and we had to move out. Instead of panicking, I called a fellow vendor, someone I admired and trusted, and suggested that we create our own collective. We had learned from experience what worked and what didn't. We were ready to build something better.

Within 30 days, she and I created "The Hive – A Pop-Up Collective." We designed the logo, filed our LLC, opened bank accounts, secured a location, and signed up other entrepreneurs, many of whom we had already cultivated relationships with. People often say starting a business is hard, and it is. However, in the United States, we are fortunate to have systems and freedoms that enable entrepreneurship. I never take that for granted. It's one of the reasons I always encourage others, especially women, either just starting out or changing lanes later in life, to permit themselves to try.

The Power of the Right Partners

Every successful entrepreneurial venture has a foundation. For The Hive, that foundation was a strong partnership. My partner and I divided responsibilities according to our strengths: She led the visual and creative aspects while I handled operations, leases, and finances. It was a division that mirrored how great businesses scale, by allowing each contributor to operate in their zone of genius. Just as important was our shared vision. We weren't building just a boutique; we were building a business model.

The most essential component of The Hive is the right mix of micro-entrepreneurs who share the space, the Showroom Partners. The Hive gives us the chance to realize our dreams of owning our own boutique without being burdened with the responsibilities that come with being a sole owner. We staff the store, bring in our own inventory, and share the responsibility of making the store thrive. We post each other's social media reels and stories. We cover for each other when needed, give advice when asked, and take the Hive brand on the road to weekend markets across the state to 3-week shopping events like the Houston Rodeo. The Showroom Partners are the heart of The Hive, and we truly share in helping create each other's successes.

Pandemic Pivots and a New Location

In June 2020, just months into the COVID-19 pandemic, my team took a bold step. While other stores were closing, I signed a three-year lease at a new location in Houston's Rice Village. To most people, it seemed like madness. But we saw an opportunity. People were hungry for connection. They were tired of isolation, of screen time, of online shopping. They wanted to touch things again, to talk to real people, to feel human. The Hive offered just that: an in-store experience rich in personality, curated inventory, and heartfelt service. Three years later, I became the sole owner of The Hive, continuing to build on its legacy with the same entrepreneurial energy I had first channeled into that motor home.

Learning by Listening

I never underestimate the power of listening. Long before I opened my doors, I listened. I listened to podcasts, joined online forums, watched what other successful retailers did, and paid attention to how customers interacted in stores. I observed how merchandise was displayed, how staff greeted customers, and what made a space feel inviting. Too many entrepreneurs fail because they assume instead of observing. I chose to listen to my partners, mentors, my peers, my customers, and even my mistakes. The Hive reflects what I've learned, borrowed, adjusted, and made my own.

What Makes the Hive Different?

Sure, we sell great fashion, jewelry, candles, bags, and gifts, but we also offer fun. You'll hear laughter in the store. You may be offered a tequila shot or a mimosa while browsing. You'll see partners chatting with customers like old friends. And sometimes, they are. Over time, strangers become regulars. Regulars become friends. Friends become collaborators. Having Showroom Partners, there's a rotating palette of fashion and lifestyle items for all ages, budgets, and tastes. Every week, the partners bring in fresh merchandise, and there is always something new to discover. And because our partners staff the shop themselves, they know the stories behind the products. They can tell you where the jewelry is made, how the handbag was sourced, or what inspired the latest collection. It's not just retail, it's a living, breathing experience. It's personal. And that's why it works. And the community has noticed. Hosting events, partnering with new brands on trunk shows, and creating memorable shopping experiences have turned The Hive into more than a store with beautiful and unique items. It's a destination and an experience.

If I could sit down with every aspiring entrepreneur over coffee, I'd share these lessons:

1. **It's Never Too Late to Reinvent.**

   Whether you're 25 or 65, there's no expiration date on a dream. Your timing is perfect when you decide to act. I launched my dream in my 50s. There is no deadline on purpose.

2. **Experience is Your Superpower.**

   All those years in commercial real estate? They gave me the foundation that many others didn't have: negotiating, marketing, and budgeting. I didn't waste my past; I repurposed it. And don't forget that age is knowledge. I might not have a long list of credits or letters behind my name, but I do have a PhD in Real Life Experiences!

3. **Start Small, But Start.**

   Don't wait for perfection. Start with what you have. The fashion truck was humble, but it provided me with proof of concept and a customer base. It allowed me to make mistakes, learn from them, and adjust before going "big" with a storefront.

4. **Don't Pretend to Know It All.**

   Asking for help isn't a weakness; it's wisdom. Admitting to inexperience opens doors. Pride closes them. You will be surprised how many people will be honored to share their knowledge with you.

5. **Partnerships Multiply Possibility.**

    Choosing the right business partner and/or partners can be transformational. Complementary strengths and mutual respect create momentum that solo entrepreneurs often struggle to maintain alone.

6. **Listen More Than You Talk.**

    Pay attention. Your customers will tell you what they want - if you're willing to hear them. Observing what works (and what doesn't) is a goldmine of entrepreneurial data.

7. **Culture Isn't a Buzzword - It's the Brand.**

    People come back to The Hive not just for our affordable and on-trend inventory, but also for how the store makes them feel. That vibe - warm, fun, supportive, caring - isn't accidental. It's genuine because we love what we are doing, and it shows.

8. **Build with Others, Not Alone.**

    Entrepreneurship is lonely only if you let it be. Our Showroom Partners function like an advisory board. We give each other feedback, test ideas, and lift each other up. We also invite other small businesses or start-ups to "pop up" in our store. That mentoring spirit keeps things fresh and reciprocal.

A Shoutout to the Team

Every woman who walks in as a partner brings something special. They're not vendors. I hate that word. Vendors sound transactional. Partners sound invested. And they are. They help manage the store. They support one another. They work together on displays. The Hive thrives because we collaborate, building off each other's ideas and strengths. We value the support system offered because we are all not just entrepreneurs, but solopreneurs. These women are creative, gritty, generous, and driven. Watching them succeed is one of the most rewarding aspects of this journey.

What My Dad Taught Me

My dad was my first mentor. He taught my brother, sister, and me about money, time, and integrity. He made sure we knew how to save, protect our credit, invest our money, and show up on time. "If you're not 15 minutes early, you're late," he'd say. That stuck.

He also taught us to take pride in our work and to learn continually. That's why I'm such a big advocate for self-education today. With YouTube, social media, podcasts, and eBooks like this one, there's no excuse not to know how to set up an LLC, track your expenses, or understand your taxes.

Looking Forward

In July 2025, The Hive celebrated five years in Rice Village. That's no small feat in a world where many boutiques barely survive their first year. The Hive has not only endured; it has thrived. And why? Because at its core, it is a place of reinvention for its founder, for its partners, and for its customers. It proves that entrepreneurship is not about having it all figured out. It's about starting with what you have, learning as you go, and building with others who share your vision and passion.

My journey is proof that your dream doesn't have an expiration date, and neither does your impact. Whether you're driving a fashion truck across Houston or opening a storefront in a pandemic, the only question that matters is this:

Are you ready to begin?

The Value of Purposeful Living
No wind is favorable to a sailor without a rudder.
No life is favorable to a person without purpose.

Setting up your day with Purposeful Living by defining your Intentions, what you are grateful for, how you want to interact, and what you want to create for the day will help you remove distractions and stay focused. Purposeful Living is about aligning your actions, goals, and values with a more profound sense of purpose. It's the conscious choice to live each day intentionally, focusing on what truly matters rather than drifting through the day without direction.

Each day is a brand new, never-before-used baby day.
What can I bring to the day?

BETH BRANIFF HARP

Beth Braniff Harp has spent more than thirty years leading with purpose, compassion, and an unwavering commitment to Houston's most vulnerable children. As **Chief Executive Officer of Kids' Meals, Inc.**, she oversees the nation's only home meal delivery program serving preschool-aged children living in food-insecure homes. Under her leadership, the organization has evolved from a small grassroots effort into a powerful movement that nourishes children, supports families, and strengthens communities.

Beth is recognized for her visionary approach to leadership and her ability to unite people around a shared mission. She believes that ending childhood hunger begins with building healthier families and connected neighborhoods. With a blend of strategy and empathy, she has built partnerships and programs that create lasting impact.

She also founded the organization's annual **Harvest Luncheon**, a cherished community event honoring those dedicated to the fight against childhood hunger.

Before joining Kids' Meals, Beth served with **Child Advocates, Inc.**, amplifying the voices of abused and neglected children, and later directed sponsorships for the **Houston Children's Festival**, one of the largest events of its kind in the nation.

Guided by her belief that every child deserves to be seen, fed, and given the opportunity to flourish, Beth continues to lead with heart and purpose.

bharp@kids
MealsInc.org

CHAPTER 12

BUILDING MORE THAN MEALS: MY JOURNEY WITH KIDS' MEALS

By Beth Harp

I never planned to become the leader of a nonprofit. I never envisioned directing the construction of a 60,000-square-foot facility or growing an organization from four employees and two vans, one barely running, to over 50 team members and a fleet delivering more than 9,000 meals a day. But here I am, sixteen years in, still learning, still leading, and still humbled by the mission. If there's anything I can offer as a mentor to someone starting their own business or nonprofit, it's this: don't wait for perfect clarity. Follow the pull of purpose. You'll find your path along the way.

Let me take you back to the beginning because every story, especially those rooted in service, deserves context.

From Public Relations to Public Service

I began my professional journey in PR and marketing, working for an ad agency in Dallas after college. When I got engaged and moved back to Houston, I had no plans to jump into nonprofit work. But sometimes, the seeds are planted long before we realize we're standing in a field of purpose. My mother had founded Child Advocates in 1983, right around our kitchen table. It was a grassroots effort to bring advocacy to abused and neglected children. By 1990, when I returned to Houston, she asked me to help out for six months. "Just help with PR and events," she said.

I thought I was doing her a favor. But really, she was introducing me to my calling.

That six-month stint turned into nine years. I had to go through formal interviews and reporting structures after all, I was the founder's daughter, but it turned out to be the best professional education I could have asked for. The mission soaked into me. The passion for service took root. I realized I could never go back to work that wasn't purpose-driven.

The Festival Years and Finding My Voice

After my full-time tenure at Child Advocates, I transitioned into a contract role managing the Houston Children's Festival, a massive undertaking that eventually became the largest children's festival in the country. My job included event direction, fundraising, marketing, and spokesperson duties. I loved it. It allowed me to merge my media background with my heart for advocacy.

Those years taught me how to connect with donors, corporate sponsors, and media partners while staying fiercely focused on the mission. I developed relationships across the city. I learned how to tell stories that moved people into action. Most importantly, I learned how to raise funds without losing integrity, something every nonprofit leader must master.

The Unexpected Call: A New Chapter Begins

In 2009, I got a call from my brother, Jack. He told me about an organization called Kids' Meals. It was in the process of reforming after its former leadership had failed it. The mission was powerful, delivering healthy meals directly to the homes of preschool-aged children living in food-insecure environments. Jack asked me to meet with the new executive director, Ruth.

Ruth was a force of nature. Her passion was electric. When she spoke about hungry kids, it wasn't abstract; it was urgent, real, personal. She invited me on a ride-along to deliver meals. That day changed me.

We drove to a trailer park in Independence Heights. As we pulled in, children began chasing the van, toddlers, preschoolers, barefoot, bright-eyed, hungry. Little ones waited on makeshift steps for their only meal of the day. I had worked in nonprofits for years, but I had never seen this kind of poverty in my own city.

It took my breath away. And I knew I had to be part of this.

Jumping In with Both Feet

At first, I was hired on contract to do grant writing, PR, and events. The organization didn't have any events when I started. We had one functional van, a staff of four, and almost no community awareness. I saw that as an opportunity, not a problem.

What followed was a whirlwind of creativity, hustle, and trust. I was given the freedom to build and connect. I called every contact I had. I crafted new ways to tell our story. I met people like Peter Remington who saw the potential and stepped in to help elevate our message.

We were serving 800 meals a day when I started. Today, we deliver over 9,400 meals a day, and when school is out, we feed older siblings, too, because hunger doesn't stop at age five. During the summers and holidays, we now feed over 16,000 children daily. That's a miracle, and it's also a result of strategic growth, relentless vision, and community partnership.

Building a Team with Purpose

In the beginning, we were just trying to keep things moving. But as we grew, I learned the importance of investing in people. From the drivers we call "hope providers" to our leadership team, everyone needs to feel seen, heard, and valued.

I learned to hire not just for skills, but for heart. Passion for the mission had to shine through in interviews. We now do team interviews, thorough background checks, and shared training across departments. Whether you're the CFO or a new development coordinator, your first days will include packing meals, riding delivery routes, and sitting down with team leads. Why? Because culture is contagious and ours is centered on empathy and excellence.

We've grown from a team of four to 51 employees and 24 vans. We have a Director of HR now, but even before that, we trained with intention. Our staff knows their role in the bigger picture. They know that feeding a child is more than handing off a sandwich; it's helping them meet critical developmental milestones and keeping their brain healthy so they can learn, grow, and thrive.

The Big Build: From Scarcity to Scale

I never set out to build a facility. But necessity is the mother of all transformation.

We were maxed out. Our tiny space could no longer accommodate our growth. So we dreamed bigger. Together with our board, we cast a vision for a 60,000-square-foot facility that could allow us to triple our impact and serve more than 26,000 meals a day by 2031.

I didn't know how to build a building. But I knew how to ask for help. I leaned into our board, which brought in expertise from construction, architecture, real estate, and project management. We formed committees. We built it step-by-step. There were challenges, of course, financial, operational, and emotional, but we kept our eye on the mission.

And soon, we'll open the doors to a one-of-a-kind building that will become a national model for childhood hunger relief.

Lessons for Future Leaders

People often say I'm not an entrepreneur. Maybe I didn't start a business in the traditional sense, but I built something from scratch. I took a broken organization and helped turn it into a thriving, trusted institution. That spirit, that courage to build, pivot, and lead, is what entrepreneurship is all about.

If I were mentoring someone who wanted to start their own nonprofit or business, I'd offer these key lessons:

1. **Build a strong advisory board** with a diversity of perspectives. Their counsel is priceless.
2. **Create a plan, a real**, measurable strategic plan. It's your North Star.
3. **Invest in people.** Identify their gifts and give them room to grow.
4. **Treat donors and volunteers like customers.** Your organization doesn't exist without them. Communicate consistently. Make them feel part of the mission.
5. **Prioritize ROI.** Not every opportunity deserves your time. Focus on the initiatives that yield the greatest impact.

6. **Use KPIs to guide your progress.** They help you track growth, prove efficiency, and communicate impact clearly to stakeholders.
7. **Be flexible and resilient.** The weather, the economy, and even pandemics, things will change. You have to pivot and plan for contingencies.
8. **Embrace technology.** It changes fast, but staying current helps you scale your message and your mission.

What I'm Most Proud Of

I get asked a lot, "What's your proudest moment?" It's hard to choose. But one moment stands out.

Recently, we were in the back of our building doing our team huddle. Someone led a quote of the day, we did our daily cheer, and I looked around at this team, this family. People from every walk of life, united by one mission: to serve hungry children. And I stepped back, tears in my eyes, and just whispered, "Thank you, Lord."

I am proud of our new facility. I'm proud that Kids' Meals is now a household name. But more than anything, I'm proud of the culture we've built, one rooted in compassion, excellence, and purpose.

A Final Word to Fellow Builders

If you are reading this and thinking of starting your own thing, whether it's a business or a nonprofit, let me tell you this: You don't have to know everything. But you do have to care deeply. Care enough to learn. Care enough to build wisely. Care enough to stay when things get hard.

You are not just launching an idea, you are creating something that could change lives. So surround yourself with people who sharpen you.

Keep your mission front and center. And never forget, the smallest acts, like a peanut butter sandwich delivered to a child, can spark the biggest change.

We didn't just build Kids' Meals. We built a movement. And you can, too!

ALICIA JANSEN

Alicia is a speaker, writer, and founder of **Grateful Unicorn**, an inspirational company dedicated to helping others heal from life's hurts by walking hand in hand with God. Her journey is a testament to the power of faith, gratitude, and resilience. Through her writing and speaking, she transforms her own struggles into stories of hope—turning her "mess into a message" and inspiring others to live with purpose, one day at a time.

With grace, humor, and authenticity, Alicia encourages others to find peace amid chaos and to see God's light even in difficult moments. Her heartfelt teachings remind readers that every challenge holds an opportunity for growth and that faith can turn pain into purpose.

Drawing on more than thirty years of professional leadership experience and a lifetime of personal transformation, she brings wit, wisdom, and practical faith-based insights to everyday life—both at work and at home.

Alicia finds renewal in nature, where she listens for God's whispers in the rustling of trees and birdsong. Her message is simple yet profound: live with gratitude, walk in grace, and share God's love, compassion, and patience with the world—one intentional step at a time.

> "What would you attempt to do if you knew you could not fail?"
>
> –Robert H. Schuller

CHAPTER 13

A LOVE LETTER

By Alicia Jansen

When **I was** growing up, I truly believed God planted a light in my soul. A light that would be turned up brightly and dimmed down often. As we walk through life, there are people, situations, and events that will shape us. These experiences can traumatize us and make us fearful, or they can lift us and make us strong. When I was young, my mother passed away suddenly. It caused me to be fearful of commitment. To avoid pain, I became a people pleaser and a control freak. Addiction in my family became a coping mechanism. My grandmother was my lifeline as she introduced me to God and taught me resilience.

My personal and professional life took many twists and turns that would continue to build my character. Experiences such as graduating from college, getting married, being laid off, being promoted, and losing people I love to disease. Over time, these experiences didn't just pass through my life—they shaped it. Each moment, each challenge, each unexpected blessing offered a piece of wisdom that slowly transformed how I lived, led, and loved. The stories that follow are the moments where wisdom stepped in and redirected me.

For example, I realized that in order to become a better leader, a better wife, and a better person, I needed to strengthen my inner fortitude. I showed up for my team and my friends whenever they needed leadership, encouragement, or a push forward—but I wasn't always offering that same support to myself.

One of the most transformative shifts in my growth came from learning to rewrite the narrative in my own mind. It was far too easy to be critical, impatient, or unkind when I missed a deadline or fell short of my expectations. But choosing to speak to myself with the same encouragement, empowerment, and grace that I gave to others changed everything. I was becoming my own best friend.

With every trauma and triumph along the way, I began to see that each moment, whether painful or beautiful, carried a lesson and a blessing. Life kept offering me choices: I could sit in the shade of what I'd been through, or I could rise, step into the sun, and let those lessons shape me into the person God wanted me to be.

And in that choosing, I discovered something sacred: every experience becomes a chapter in a love letter from life itself.

These stories, these bits of hard-earned wisdom, are my love letter—to myself and to anyone who longs to embrace life fully, turn up the light within them, and grow into the person they dream of becoming. May this letter be your reminder that peace can be found even in the chaos, one brave, intentional choice at a time.

Never Compare

We consciously or unconsciously seek the approval of others. When I look to external reference points like people, situations, or objects to boost me up, I let my ego and false sense of power drive me. But this ego-based "power" only lasts as long as those things last. When I lost my job because of a new CEO and lost my house due to a hurricane, I no longer had the title or materialistic things that I based my influence or power on – it was gone.

Don't look outside for validation, look inside to your God-given spirit. Your spirit isn't influenced by objects, situations, circumstances, people, or things. Your spirit is immune to these things; it is humble, not fearful, it is respectful, it is kind, it does not judge. You are not above or below anyone. If someone has more than you, be happy for them. Wish them well. Let this saying boost you every day: "Today, I will judge no one". That includes yourself.

Your Choice

I have felt many times that something or someone "made" me feel or react in a certain way. I blamed others for their actions (or lack of) and how it shifted my personal life or career. I wanted to blame or point the finger at someone or something instead of taking responsibility. When I feel frustrated or upset by a person or situation, I have empowered them to make me feel a certain way.

You have a choice every day about how you react and act in every situation. You can't control others or their free will, but you can control what feelings you have attached to it. If you don't like how you feel, change it. You choose what you say, how you say it, how you feel about it, and what to do next. You can change the course of what happens next. The situation doesn't get to decide for you.

Let Go, Let God

When we feel things don't go our way, it is often due to someone or some situation that didn't meet our expectations. They didn't play the role we expected, and they didn't stay in the box we built. We try to control the outcome based on what we want to happen. I can be happy or excited about the outcome if my expectations are met or exceeded. I can become disappointed, sad, or angry if my expectations are not met. I want to fix it, and I believe I have a better solution. This isn't about lowering your expectations but setting realistic ones.

Since you can't fix or control anyone, practice detaching from the outcome. You can encourage and influence someone to move in a certain direction, but it is their choice. The only person that you can control or fix is yourself. A great reminder is a line in the Serenity Prayer "… taking this sinful world as it is, not as I would have it,…" because you are not in control of the outcome or consequences from someone else's actions. However, you can set a great example by modeling the way with your actions and words. So let it go and give it to God. Your part is to hold God's hand and let Him gently mold you into the person He created you to be.

Today's a Good Day to Hold God's Hand

There have been many days that I jump out of bed with a never-ending to-do list. Or I had a disagreement with someone, or something didn't go my way, and my first thought is "ugh, I have to deal with this now." We can be overwhelmed before our feet hit the ground.

Your mindset in the morning can determine your day, and your mindset at night can determine your dreams. You may not have the answers to solve the challenges you face, but give your burdens, your fears, your anxiety to God first thing in the morning and let Him carry them. Squeeze God's hand and ask that He walk with you today. What you say to yourself sets the tone, so tell yourself, "expect great things and great things will happen." This hopeful approach will prepare your mind and heart to be excited about the possibilities, rather than dread the unknown. Before you drift off to sleep, thank God for the day and release any remaining fear, negative feelings, or burdens to Him and let Him sleep on it, not you.

Grounded in Gratitude

When I take my eyes off of God and try to fix things myself, I tend to find what is wrong in the situation. I can spot it immediately and speak my mind about what is not working according to my plan. It is easy for us to focus on what is wrong and miss what is right.

You can't be stressed if you feel blessed. Every day, be thankful for what God has given you. Find the beauty around you, such as the birds singing and the sunshine. Thank Him for the roof over your head and food on the table. Thank Him for the gifts he has given you in your career and in your personal life.

Be grateful that He has given you the skills to be a leader, to have a compassionate heart, and a desire to serve others. Be thankful for the situations and people He places in your path to teach you. Every experience is a lesson. There will be people and events in your life that cause pain, disappointment, hurt, and anger. And there will be people and events in your life that will bring you great joy, peace, calmness, and love. Each lesson teaches you something, what to do or not do, about moving forward in this journey. Even if the lesson hurts, be grateful. Be grateful for every day on this earth, even for the days that leave scars.

Stop, Pause, and Pray

When something takes you by surprise, it is easy to react negatively or say something you regret. Or it may make you freeze in your tracks. I have had many sleepless nights wondering if only I had said something different or acted in a certain way, things would have turned out better, or at least in my favor. But I didn't take time to think before my mouth flew open or my heart shut down.

Before reacting to any person or situation, make a mental stop. Pause and pray, even if only for a nanosecond. This gives your mind and heart a break to think and let God step in. You still may not make it perfect, but your next words or actions won't be a knee-jerk reaction. Give yourself a moment to breathe and your mind to catch up. Give God a chance to guide your next move. Walk away from the situation with your head held high because God was in the mix.

One Day at a Time

It can be difficult to let go of the past. Traumas, hurts, and hang-ups can follow us around and keep us stuck. It is hard to let go of the pain. It can be just as hard not to worry about the future. Anxiety and fear can creep in as you run different "what if" scenarios in your mind. What if I don't get the job? What if my loved one doesn't get better? What if I can never forgive that person?

Remember the saying "Yesterday is history, tomorrow is a mystery, but today is a gift. That is why it is called the present." You can't change the past. Repeat this saying often if your mind starts to walk backwards, "don't look back, you are not going that way." You can plan for the future, but believe God is moving mountains for your utmost good. What you have is this moment. Find beauty around you. Catch your wandering mind and be present during the different situations happening around you. Pray so you can bring your best to the day. Great encouragement comes from the Serenity Prayer, "living one day at a time; enjoying one moment at a time." If your mind is consumed with the past or worried about the future, you can't experience the wonders or the lessons that God has for you within these 24 hours.

Give Yourself Grace

We can be our own worst critics. However, we often won't hesitate to be a cheerleader for other people. It is so easy to talk negatively to ourselves. We may even say hurtful things, such as you are not worthy, you are not talented, or you are an imposter. When I procrastinate, I beat myself up. When a friend needs comfort or an encouraging word, I am there in a flash. Why can't I do that for myself?

God doesn't talk to you that way. He asks that we love ourselves and each other. Don't make excuses, but give yourself permission to be imperfect. Give yourself grace, encouragement, and empowerment. Remember to fill your cup up with God's words for you. He calls you His child; you are chosen.

You are loved. If you stumble, brush yourself off, straighten your crown, and get up. Grab God's hand and let Him lift you to your feet. Even if it is only a small step, celebrate it. Start writing an encouraging journal to yourself, treating yourself like a friend. You can choose to shift your mindset and your actions at this moment. Make your next word or move a positive one.

Allow Others to Straighten Your Crown

I am programmed, like many, to think first of family and friends versus myself. This mindset keeps me in a state of constant productivity with a never-ending to-do list. I will always wear multiple hats in my life, and I will put pressure on myself to perform many roles. One of those roles is being a friend, easily offering my talent and time to others. It is a measure of self-worth and gives me a sense of control. Where am I on this list?

My cousin works for a major airline, and he reminds me there's a reason why passengers are asked to put their oxygen mask on first. He explains that most women disagree with this because women want to take care of friends or family first. His response always hits me in the heart - you can't help anybody if you're dead. If I don't take care of myself, emotionally, physically, and spiritually, I will not be the best version of myself. When I help others, I view it as an honor. But I've learned that when I'm the one in need, I must view it the same way. Allowing others to help me is also an honor for *them*. To truly be a gracious giver, I have to learn how to be a gracious receiver.

Allow people to straighten your crown. Allow them to reciprocate with their time and talent. You can do anything in this world, you just don't have to do it all by yourself. Receive their generosity with grace and gratitude. Don't be afraid to raise your hand.

It is ok to ask for a lifeline. No one is a mind reader, so give them the decoder ring. Tell them what it is you need to be successful, happy, and balanced. It doesn't make you weak; it highlights your strength. It models the way for others to realize that support starts with giving people permission to help.

Invite Your Inner Child to a Playdate

We often get caught up in the day-to-day of being responsible. We tell our inner child to sit down and be quiet; we have work to do. Later, we can play. As a child, it was easier to laugh, to be curious, and to find beauty in the everyday. We didn't know about taking ourselves too seriously.

Let the inner child out to play. Hold her hand and let her take you on a walk through nature. Laugh at the little things and let her smile be contagious. Be curious about people and make new friends.

Look for the light in what we have in common vs the shadows in our differences. Let her tell you about her dreams and passions. Let her read to you what lights her imagination. Ask her to never sit down and always raise her hand. Put your playdates on your daily calendar.

Play Nice in the Sandbox

At a leadership retreat, the book we read reminded us to play nice in the sandbox. Lead the way by collaborating with others, lending a helping hand, and being part of the solution. As I was climbing the corporate ladder, it wasn't just the functional skills that led to a promotion but my approach to the job. At this company, your emotional intelligence was just as important as your IQ. Not everyone I met on that journey felt the same way. They worked their way to the top without help, and they expected me to do the same.

Build your reputation by paying forward what you have learned. You stand on the shoulders of others before you. Share your wisdom and insights, be a team player, and don't kick sand in someone's eyes. Steven Covey's The Seven Habits of Effective People mentions "seek first to understand, then to be understood."

God gave you two ears and one mouth so you would listen more than you speak. He asks that we treat each other with kindness, compassion, empathy, understanding, tolerance, and grace. The late Maya Angelou said, "I've learned that people will forget what you said, they will forget what you did, but they will never forget how you made them feel." Treat people as you want to be treated.

You are Not Alone
When we rush through this life, it is easy to lean only on ourselves. If something doesn't go well, it is easy to isolate. You may feel shame or guilt over something that happened, and you put on a mask to protect yourself. When I have walked beside a loved one's addiction journey, I have hidden so no one will know my pain.

You are never alone. God is standing right next to you, holding out His hand. Grab it. He has assigned a guardian angel to be by your side every moment you walk this earth. Let this angel whisper in your ear. Be still and know you are surrounded by love and protection. He places people in your path as his earth angels. These are the people who are in your corner, no matter what. They accept you as you are, occasionally offering tough love.

God is doing His work through these people. These encounters are a God Thing and not a coincidence. It was meant to be. When a song hits your heart a certain way, it was meant to happen. When a friend says the right words, God made sure you were ready to listen. Lean into God and know you never walk through this life alone.

ROMAIN KAPADIA

Romain Kapadia is an entrepreneur, investor, and global adventurer who has spent more than two decades building businesses and living life on his own terms. Growing up an only child, he developed a fierce independence and resilience that have guided his journey across industries and continents.

Romain launched his first venture in the early 2000s—a men's luxury fashion brand that gained international acclaim, worn by cultural icons including Jared Leto, Ricky Martin, and David Bowie. Today, he serves as **Managing Partner of Founder's Capital**, a New York–based private equity firm that acquires and scales founder-led consumer businesses across the United States. He is also the Co-Founder of a rapidly growing events and entertainment company headquartered in the Southwest.

In 2023, Romain faced his greatest personal test when he was diagnosed with Stage 3 cancer, later advancing to Stage 4. After enduring multiple surgeries and treatments, he continues to live with courage and gratitude, sharing his journey through **@247manifesto** to inspire others facing life's toughest battles.

A lifelong explorer, Romain has traveled to more than seventy countries across all seven continents, completed over a dozen international marathons, supports startups as an angel investor, and still chases waves in search of the world's best undiscovered surf towns.

"The journey of a thousand miles begins with a single step."

–Lao Tzo

CHAPTER 14

FROM DREAMER TO DOER

By Romain Kapadia

I've always been a dreamer. Growing up as an only child, without siblings to guide or influence me, I spent long stretches alone, lost in thought. I learned to think independently, letting my imagination run wild.

My dad, an immigrant in the 60s from India and a graduate of one of its top engineering universities, was my earliest role model. I watched him work tirelessly in the corporate world, supporting our family and building a new life from scratch. Over time, however, I saw how the long hours, the constant pressure, and the slow grind wore him down. That spark and ambition I once admired began to fade.

These experiences left a mark.

As I entered my teenage years and began exploring what I wanted to do professionally, I started noticing a pattern that the people around me who seemed to be the most energized and fulfilled, and whose lives I wanted to emulate, were business owners. Entrepreneurs. Their pursuits combined a sense of independence and unlimited possibilities that energized a dreamer like me.

Witnessing my own father's struggles, I realized that the traditional 9-to-5 could never offer the freedom or sense of purpose I craved. Despite the expectations of the conservative Indian community that I was raised in, where success was typically defined by careers in medicine or engineering, I knew early on that if I wanted to build a meaningful life on my own terms, I'd have to create it myself.

So, I did.

Early Startup Lessons

While still in college and itching to launch my first venture and start generating real income, I began looking for a product that didn't exist in the U.S. market but solved a clear problem. That line of thinking led me to a surprising place, my bathroom, for a simple tool I used daily–a stainless steel tongue scraper. Common in India and widely valued for its oral health benefits, it had been a regular part of my routine since childhood, something passed down from my parents. Yet despite its proven benefits, it was practically nonexistent in the American consumer market. That gap became my opportunity.

I started cold-calling local machine shops to explore how I could produce it. Eventually, I found a partner willing to take a chance. I skillfully negotiated a deal where we'd skip the upfront mold costs. Instead, I would give him a percentage of each unit sold. It was my first real taste of creative deal-making.

We built a simple website, started cold-calling grocery stores, and slowly got traction. Eventually, we sold several thousand units through a local chain and our online store.

While it wasn't the windfall I had imagined, it was my first real taste of entrepreneurship. It taught me a valuable lesson that I carry to this day: that changing consumer behavior, especially in something as habitual and personal as oral care, is incredibly hard. But it also taught me something deeper: action trumps ideas. By just getting started, I could adapt as I went along and leverage early momentum into bigger opportunities. I crystallized this experience as I thought about my next venture.

Bright Lights, Big City

In the Spring of 1998, I graduated from the University of Texas with a BBA in Marketing with two job offers: The first with Neiman Marcus in their, at the time, fledgling dotcom division and, the second, a fashion importer in Houston where I'd work directly with the company President, exposing me to all parts of the apparel business from design, production, operations, logistics, marketing and finance. With my mind set on NYC to chase my fashion entrepreneurship dream, I chose the latter. Whilst I learned a lot, my restlessness only grew, so a year later, with no job, no contacts, and no place to stay, I purchased a one-way ticket and left with two suitcases and a boatload of ambition to make it in the Big Apple.

Hustle Town

NYC was a difficult start. After six long months of job hunting, I finally accepted a role at a well-known youth apparel brand. The date? September 11, 2001.

That morning, I traveled on a train underneath the World Trade Center, just between the first and second plane strikes. I rushed to my office on 34th Street and watched the towers fall. It was a harrowing, surreal moment. Witnessing the city's resilience in the days and weeks that followed, though, only deepened my conviction that I had made the right move. New York's grit and determination to rebuild became a source of inspiration as I mustered my own courage to one day start my own label.

I started small, walking the streets of the garment district during my lunch hours, memorizing the collection of stores on each block—35th street sold leathers, 38th street sold accessories, 39th and 40th street sold fabrics, etc. Simultaneously, eager to make connections, I started attending industry events and volunteering at Gen Art, a non-profit organization that supported up-and-coming creatives in film, fashion, and the arts.

One night while volunteering, I unsuspectingly handed a gift bag to a magazine editor, and upon his asking about what I did, I boldly lied to him, boasting I was an "up-and-coming" menswear designer. He gave me his business card and told me to send him an email.

I spent the next two weeks sketching ideas to share with the editor, which, to my surprise, he agreed to feature in his next issue. Shortly thereafter, things quickly snowballed.

Unbeknownst to me, someone reading the article nominated me for the "Best New Menswear Designer" award by The Fashion Group International, a prestigious industry award recognizing new talent. A few weeks later, I was announced as a Finalist and my name was published, alongside the other finalists in the industry's leading publication, WWD. Unfortunately, my boss also read the same paper and, upon seeing the article, he abruptly called me into his office.

A few days later, I quit my job.

Less than twelve months after arriving in the city, my label, Romain Kapadia New York, was born.

The Illusion of Success

When faced with the daunting reality of being unemployed, I had to ask myself: what now? I began by visiting the same fabric stores and factories I used to frequent during lunch breaks, this time to talk about making samples. I reached out to the Italian Trade

Commission to explore connections with overseas manufacturers. Over the course of several weeks, I created my first mini collection, twelve pieces in total.

Next came the hard part–selling.

I obtained my first orders by walking into well-known downtown stores with two suitcases full of samples, unannounced and insisting on speaking with the buyer. Eventually, as awareness for my line grew, by 2003, I was able to hire multiple sales showrooms, a PR agent, and began attending trade shows. The business exploded with distribution expanding to over 50 top retailers globally. Through the years, we generated millions of dollars in revenue, were the recipients of over a dozen prestigious industry awards, and received substantial press coverage from GQ, Vogue, Maxim, FHM, and others. Celebrity clients included Jared Leto, Ricky Martin, and David Bowie.

From the outside, it looked like a success. And for a while, it was. But the deeper reality started to set in, the relentless hours, the cash flow struggles, the hand-to-mouth existence, coupled with the vanity and volatility of the fashion industry. By late 2008, I found myself wondering: What's next?

Slowly, I began to distance myself from the business. What I had worked for and dreamt about for so long turned out not to be the thing that fulfilled me. I began the search for a new identity.

The Reinvention

By 2009, I knew I needed to hit reset. I had spent nearly a decade in fashion and achieved more than I had imagined, but emotionally and financially, it wasn't sustainable. I wanted to build something more lasting, more aligned with my evolving values.

So, I shut it down. At the time, it was perhaps the hardest decision of my life.

I knew I needed to completely reinvent myself, and I believed the best path forward was through an MBA. It would give me exposure to new opportunities, time to reflect on what I truly wanted, and access to a network of new ideas and people. I set my sights on getting into a top-tier program. The application process was intense. I took the GMAT twice and learned Spanish in just six weeks to meet the second-language requirement of my top choice, INSEAD, one of the world's leading global MBA programs. At 32, I was older than most of my classmates, but that turned out to be a strength. I brought real-world, bootstrapped, entrepreneurial experience into the classroom, something most of my peers hadn't yet encountered.

It was exactly what I needed.

The Comeback

Upon graduation in 2010, I joined a tech startup run by my peers. It was a flash-sale platform focused on college students, think Gilt meets campus life. I joined as the Marketing & Business Development Director. We scaled the business fast, with hundreds of product partners and thousands of customers, raised venture capital, and eventually sold to a competitor. It wasn't a headline-making sale, but it was a masterclass in startup growth, fundraising, and an exit.

From there, in 2014, I partnered with a friend and professional contact, a senior Private Equity executive, to set up a new investment platform as an independent sponsor, a branch of Private Equity that raises capital on a deal-by-deal basis to acquire companies. That exposure broadened my experience across dozens of industries beyond fashion and retail. I learned how to deal with investors, structure deals, sit on boards, and negotiate acquisitions.

Those lessons would soon come full circle.

Thriving Through Adversity

Around the same time that I started the Private Equity business, I was contacted by a childhood friend who owned a successful restaurant/bar and was interested in developing a standalone event hall for large gatherings. While he found the site and led the design, I wrote the business plan, raised the equity and debt capital, and collectively our group launched the business in 2015.

The first few years were tough. I took no salary for five years, as every customer deposit went straight to covering payroll and bank loans. Thankfully, demand was strong, and we quickly became one of the top event venues in the area. Eyeing expansion, we started discussions to acquire the region's leading catering company in 2017, and to build a 2nd venue in 2018. By 2019, we were ready and eager to move forward with our plans…we took out a personally guaranteed loan to buy out our investors (nearly 40 in total) to take control of the business.

Then, less than a few months later, COVID hit. No events. No revenue. Just a massive, multi-million-dollar loan, rent, and payroll to pay.

Through scrappiness, determination, and a bit of luck, we survived and came out stronger. In 2020, we completed the acquisition of the catering company. In 2021, we signed leases for two additional venues. And in 2022, we had our strongest year-to-date.

However, what I was most proud of was the commitment of our team. In an industry decimated by the pandemic, we didn't lose a single employee. Today, we're a profitable business with rapid growth and no end in sight. This success has been a culmination of the learnings from the many entrepreneurial endeavors I have had to date, including understanding customer behavior, product design, branding, fundraising, operations, and scaling.

Putting It All Together

Today, I manage an 8-figure business and negotiate 9-figure acquisitions. It's been an exciting, non-traditional, and non-linear path to entrepreneurial success. And while every chapter has been different, there have been consistent themes and universal lessons throughout my journey. These are five core principles I share with new entrepreneurs:

1. **Bias for Action** – Don't wait for the perfect plan. Start today. There are so many unanticipated situations when starting a business that you can only learn through experience. You'll learn, iterate, and gain confidence along the way, all things you won't gain by watching from the sidelines and waiting for the "right" moment.

2. **Master Your Emotions** – It's a cliché, but entrepreneurship is an emotional rollercoaster filled with only two feelings, according to Marc Andreessen–euphoria and terror. The more you can master your mind and emotions, the better equipped you'll be to weather the storm. Remember the adage "things are never as good or bad as they seem". Almost every situation is neutral except for the meaning we've attached to it.

3. **Persevere** – Grit beats IQ every time. The people who make it are the ones who just won't stop. Be relentless.

4. **Choose Partners Wisely** – Your business partner is your second spouse, who you'll likely spend more time with than your actual spouse. Be cautious, deliberate, and make sure your values align before you commit.

5. **Be the Best at Something** – Decades ago, businesses depended on product diversification to build scale. However, it's impossible to be excellent at everything, so diversification often leads to mediocrity. Today, with the internet, businesses can easily be copied and scaled lightning fast, so it's important

you focus on being the best at something to establish your competitive moat. Start narrow and dominate your niche. Find your unique square on the chessboard.

Final Thoughts

The lessons I've learned as an entrepreneur continue to guide me personally as well, especially now.

Most recently, I was diagnosed with Stage 4 cancer. Facing this disease, I've discovered many of the learnings from my entrepreneurial journey have helped me survive and thrive in the face of uncertainty, regulating my emotions, making decisions with imperfect information, and understanding that when solving complex, multi-stage problems like beating cancer, all that matters is getting to the next step.

This new reality has also forced me to be radically honest with myself and with the world, as it's a condition that I can't hide. This transparency has brought back that sense of freedom, fearlessness, and confidence that I know will also be helpful in my business endeavors, something that I had in my early 20s when I moved to New York alone, with just two suitcases in hand, ready to take on the world.

To anyone contemplating this path, all I can say is DO IT. Even if you fail, you would have grown personally, and you would have learned to pick yourself up so that you can try again, and again, and again…until you finally succeed.

Follow my journey @ Instagram.com/247manifesto.

JOSEPH G. MACHOL

Joe Machol is a dedicated public servant, entrepreneur, and proud patriot with a diverse career spanning aerospace, athletics, military service, and historical preservation. He holds a two-year associate degree from San Jacinto College and began his professional journey with Boeing Aerospace and Southwest Airlines.

For over 30 years, Joe has been a respected **college baseball umpire**. For a decade, he officiated **college football games in Conference USA (C-USA)**—bringing precision, integrity, and discipline to every field he worked.

Joe is the founder of **WW2 ETO Tours**, a company devoted to preserving the legacy of World War II veterans through immersive battlefield tours across Europe. His passion is personal—he proudly owns and maintains his father's original WWII Willys Jeep.

Currently, Joe serves on the **NFL chain crew** and works in **Quality Control at Ricetec**, a leader in agricultural technology. He has also served in the **Texas State Guard** for 10 years and has been an elected **City Councilman for the City of Seabrook** for over 8 years.

For the past decade, Joe has been a dedicated volunteer at the **Houston Air Show's "Heroes and Legends" tent**, honoring America's veterans. He is also the founder of the **Seabrook American Flag Initiative (SAFI)**—a grassroots effort to promote patriotism and civic pride throughout the community.

Ww2etoTours.com
Macholj59@gmail.com

CHAPTER 15

FROM THE GRIDIRON TO THE BEACHES OF NORMANDY— A JOURNEY OF LEGACY, PURPOSE, AND REMEMBRANCE

Joe Machol

My name is Joe Machol, and I'm the founder of WW2 ETO Tours—a company born not from a business plan, but from a son's devotion to his father's legacy. Over the years, I've worn many hats: entrepreneur, mentor, college baseball umpire, Division I football official, and NFL Game Clock Operator. But the title I hold most dear is this: proud son of Lieutenant Colonel Fred B. Machol, a decorated World War II veteran whose story didn't just shape my childhood, it shaped my calling.

Where It All Began: A Life on the Field.

My career didn't start in history or travel. I came up through the world of sports. I began umpiring baseball games at 16 in 1978 and started officiating high school football shortly after. Over the decades, I worked everything from Texas high school playoff games to Division I Conference USA and SWAC matchups. In 2002, I joined the NFL as a Game Clock Operator in Houston, a role I've held for 23 seasons. Along the way, I've worked:

- 7 NFC Wild Card Games
- 5 NFC Divisional Playoffs
- 2 NFC Championship Games
- 2 Super Bowls (XXXVIII and LI)

In that high-stakes world, I learned discipline, situational awareness, and what it means to perform under pressure. But my true education started long before that—at the dinner table, listening to my father.

A Father's Legacy, A Son's Purpose

Lt. Col. Fred B. Machol was a member of the U.S. Army's 5th Division, 21st Battery Field Artillery. He served with the Counterintelligence Corps (CIC) under the Advanced Section Communication Zone (ADSEC) and was trained in counter-sabotage by none other than Lord Victor Rothschild of British MI5. He landed on Utah Beach in July 1944 and drove across Europe through France, Belgium, and Germany—witnessing history as it unfolded. Fred's stories were riveting, about the men he served with, the horrors he witnessed, the Nazi SS soldiers who once captured him... and later surrendered to him. He walked into Dachau. He drove into Paris the day after V-E Day. These weren't just tales—they were living history, sitting across the table from me. In 2003, my father and I retraced his wartime footsteps through Iceland, England, and France. In 2005, we went further, France, Belgium, Germany, and the Czech Republic. I had the ultimate guide: a man who lived it.

From Personal Pilgrimage to Global Mission

When Fred passed in 2010, the question echoed in my heart: How do I honor him? I joined the Texas State Guard. I traveled back to

Europe. I wept at the Normandy American Cemetery. I stood in the foxholes at Bois Jacques. I visited Patton's grave, the courtroom of Nuremberg, the camp at Dachau, and the Eagle's Nest in the Bavarian Alps. These weren't tourist stops—they were sacred ground. Soon, friends began joining me. Then veterans. Then their children and grandchildren. What started as a journey of remembrance became a movement of connection and meaning. And so, WW2 ETO Tours was born.

WW2 ETO Tours: More Than a Trip, A Transformational Journey

This is not your average battlefield tour. I don't just guide people across Europe, I guide them through stories, through sacrifice, through history that lives on in each step we take. My travelers aren't just tourists. They're pilgrims, each carrying a name, a photo, a memory, or a question. They come seeking connections:

- A grandson honoring a grandfather he never met
- A veteran wanting to understand what came before him
- A teacher looking to bring history alive for her students

Together, we walk the same beaches, stand in the same towns, and feel the same weight of history, so that we can better understand the world we live in today and lead with greater purpose into the future. What started with my father's stories became my life's mission. And every time I stand at a memorial, or hear Taps played in a quiet European village, I remember this isn't just history, it's personal. And I'm here to help others feel that too. Entrepreneurship is often defined by innovation and risk, but for me, it's rooted in something far deeper: honor, remembrance, and a mission to serve. As the proud son of Lieutenant Colonel Fred B. Machol, a World War 2 veteran, I didn't just start a business; I answered a calling.

WW2 ETO Tours was born from a promise to preserve and share the stories of the Greatest Generation. But building this business wasn't just about offering educational tours. It was about creating something sacred, a bridge between generations, a way to walk in the footsteps of heroes and ensure their courage is never forgotten. To do that, I had to learn everything, from structuring a company that could operate overseas to forging trusted relationships with local guides, mayors, museum curators, and even regional governors across Europe. I wasn't just the founder, I was the guide, the historian, the marketer, the operations manager, and often the shoulder someone cried on when standing at a grave they'd never seen before. Every tour is more than a trip; it's a revelation. I've stood beside sons reading letters their fathers wrote from foxholes. I've watched granddaughters gently lay flowers on headstones, honoring relatives they never met. These are not transactions. These are transformations. In those moments, I lead not just with knowledge, but with heart. Because leadership isn't about being the loudest voice in the room, it's about being the most present, the most dependable. That's something I learned both on the field as a Division I and NFL official, and from my father, who led with quiet strength and unshakable conviction. Like many small businesses, the pandemic brought our mission to a halt. International travel stopped, and I faced the terrifying question: would WW2 ETO Tours survive? Would people still care? But instead of retreating, I doubled down. I reinvested in research, deepened partnerships, created virtual events, Zoom lectures, and online memorials. Because this work isn't just important, it's essential. And now, something extraordinary is happening. Young people are showing up, curious, open-hearted, hungry, to understand the past so they can shape a better future. They want to walk the beaches of Normandy, stand where history turned, and understand what courage, sacrifice, and duty truly mean. And that excites me.

Looking Ahead

I'm developing new tours, lesser-known campaigns like the Italian front, the Hurtgen Forest, the liberation of the Netherlands, and the resistance movements in France and Poland. I'm also working on partnerships with schools and veterans' groups to make these experiences accessible to those who might not have the means to travel. Because at the end of the day, this isn't just about WW2, it's about legacy. It's about making sure the names etched in white marble are never forgotten. It's about lifting others as we climb. It's about showing what it means to serve something bigger than yourself. If you had told me years ago that I'd be leading Americans through the forests of the Ardennes or the cliffs of Normandy, I might've laughed. But life has a way of preparing you, if you're paying attention.

So, if you ask me what leadership is, I'll say this: It's standing for something greater than yourself. If you ask what entrepreneurship means, I'll say: It's turning passion into purpose. And if you ask about mentorship, I'll tell you: It's the sacred duty to carry the torch and to light the path for others.

In 2003, Fred took most of his family to Europe to see where and what he did in WWII. Kathy & Bob Zimmerman and their son Matt, JoAnn Shire, Marylou Skelton, Patty Machol-Diehl & Ken Diehl and their three kids Kirsten, Jacob, and Adam, Annie Weaver, Peggy & Ron Bassett, Mike Machol and his two daughters Lauren and Molly, Carole Machol, and myself and my two sons Chris and Nick. Fred was an only child and always said he wished he had twelve brothers and sisters. Well, he got his wish. I am the baby of twelve, I have nine sisters and two brothers. We are not cheaper by the dozen!

When we got back in July of 2003 from Europe, Fred asked me to help find a WWII army jeep. Well, we searched and found one, bought it, and after restoring it, found out it was a 1946 CJ-2A. We made it work until we got another opportunity with the Bluebonnet military motor pool club. In a town near Seabrook, a gentleman was selling a 1944 Willys Jeep that he was in the middle of restoring. We looked at it, verified it was truly a 1944 Willys Jeep, and bought it. The President of the BMMP, Larry Steed, offered to trailer it to his house and restore it in March 2006. Larry and I worked quickly to restore the jeep because we had decided to present Fred with his fully restored jeep on June 12th, 2006, his 91st birthday.

A Needle in a Haystack

While sanding the hood, we found the original hood serial number was 20367811. When I told Fred what the number was, he told me to come over to his house, and he had his 16mm color movies from WWII cued up on his TV. There in the town of Sainte-Mère-Eglise was Fred standing next to his army jeep with the hood serial number 20367811. We also found the data plates for the jeep and know it rolled off the assembly line in Toledo, Ohio, on June 12th, 1944. Fred was born on June 12th, 1916. There were 640,000 jeeps built in WWII. Willy's produced around 363,000, so those are the odds. When June 12th, 2006, arrived, we presented Fred with his Willy's Jeep at his 90th birthday party. He was so happy to see the Jeep fully restored. Fred had driven this jeep in Normandy and throughout France, Belgium, Luxembourg, Germany, and Austria.

In 2017, I went to vote in the local city election for Seabrook, Texas, where I have lived since 1967. I heard there was a newly open council position, and it needed a special election. I decided to put my name on the ballot. I had one opponent, and he decided to tell people I was a nobody. Well, the night of the election, I received a phone call from our City Secretary and was informed I won by 82% of the vote, oh well for being a nobody. I served two four-year terms and just came off council in May 2025. I did this to give back to the community I grew up in and performed my civic duty. Fred would have liked that.

I met my wife in October of 2021 at my 40th high school reunion. Brenda had gone to the rival high school but showed up at our reunion. Brenda has supported my officiating and my passion for all things WWII. While at the Houston Entrepreneurs Forum, I met Peter Remington. Brenda has known Peter for many years and said I would really find him interesting. Brenda is a real go-getter and has been truly a love of my life. I want to say thank you to Brenda, who helped push me to do this book.

My name is Joe Machol. I am an entrepreneur, a mentor, and a keeper of stories. This is my mission, and I will walk it with honor, for as long as I am able.

TAFT MCWHORTER

Taft McWhorter is an acclaimed contemporary artist whose vibrant, thought-provoking works have captivated collectors and audiences worldwide. For nearly two decades, his art has been featured in galleries, hotels, and private collections across the United States, celebrated for its emotional depth, authenticity, and bold visual storytelling.

Together with his wife and business partner, **Dana**, Taft has built a creative partnership rooted in collaboration and shared purpose. Married for more than thirty years, they have raised three sons and continue to inspire each other both personally and professionally.

Taft's legacy extends beyond the canvas. Known for his generosity and mentorship, he has guided emerging artists and donated artwork to countless charitable causes, raising more than a million dollars to support community initiatives. His partnerships with major brands, including BMW, Porsche, the Houston Astros, and the Houston Texans, showcase his ability to blend art, culture, and innovation.

As a speaker and author, Taft co-published the landmark art book *50 Artists Houston* and delivered his first **TEDx Talk** on the evolution of the art world. His life and work stand as a testament to creativity, connection, and the enduring power of art to inspire change.

TaftMcWhorterart.com
Facebook.com/taft.mcwhorter
Instagram.com/taftmcwhorter

> "A true artist is not one who is inspired, but one who inspires others."
>
> –Salvador Dali.

CHAPTER 16

A LIFE BUILT ON PURPOSE, NOT PERFECTION

By Taft McWhorter

Pursuing Your Passion: A Life Built on Purpose, Not Perfection

> "Desire is the starting point of all achievement, not a hope, not a wish, but a keen pulsating desire which transcends everything."
>
> —Napoleon Hill

My Happy Place

I'm a professional visual artist. For the past 18 years, I've made a living selling my original artwork. I'm married to my best friend, Dana, and we run our art business together. We have three amazing sons Andrew, Zach, and Taylor and life is good.

I'm not just working. I'm thriving. I've built a life around something I love. My "job" doesn't feel like a job at all. I create art, I grow a business, and I live each day with intention.

I don't work typical hours. I don't dread Mondays or live for Fridays. Each day is different, and every day is an adventure. I'm in my happy place because I chose to pursue something I'm deeply passionate about.

I jumped into the art business with little experience in the art business. I didn't have much of a plan, but I knew that I was passionate about art.

The Truth About Starting

The first major roadblock to overcome is getting started. We all stare into the deep, dark forest and imagine the bad things, the obstacles, and the unknown. Because of this stifling imagery, we don't dare step one foot into the forest.

Let me be honest, I had no degree in art or business. I didn't know anyone in the art industry. I had never even attended an art exhibit before I set foot in the art business. But I had two powerful tools: **desire** and **a willingness to work**. That was enough to get started and it's all you need, too.

I pursued my passion with everything I had. And I made it work. I took one step at a time, one day at a time. I quickly learned that the deep, dark forest wasn't so scary. Once I entered the forest, I realized that the forest was actually beautiful and enticing. It was exactly what I was looking for. Once I entered the forest, I was so happy that I did.

Why Passion Changes Everything

When you pursue something that lights you up, your entire life begins to transform. Here's what I've learned:

1. **Self-Esteem Grows**

    You'll struggle in the beginning. Everyone does. But each time you overcome an obstacle, you'll grow stronger. You'll realize just how capable you are. Progress builds confidence, and confidence builds momentum.

2. **Your Circle Improves**

   When you follow your passion, you'll naturally connect with like-minded people. These relationships will become some of the wealthiest parts of your life. I'm endlessly grateful for the creative, driven, inspiring friends I've made on this journey.

3. **You Become More Aware**

   Your eyes open to a whole new way of living. You start making decisions with more intention. Gratitude increases. Joy multiplies. Life feels different because it is.

4. **You Find True Happiness**

   External success can be fleeting. True happiness comes from aligning your life with what fulfills you. When your work reflects your heart, happiness becomes a sustainable state.

Resetting Your Mindset

Research from Stanford University highlights a hidden danger in the phrase "find your passion." It makes it sound easy. But passion doesn't guarantee ease. When challenges come and they always do, many people give up.

That's why the mindset matters more than the mantra. This journey is about **fulfillment**, not fantasy. It's about building a life that reflects your values, not chasing overnight success.

You will hit roadblocks. You will feel burned out.
You will want to quit.
Don't.
Adjust your direction if you must, but never stop moving forward.
Never stop pursuing your passions.

This isn't about the destination. This is about the journey. Embrace all of the aspects of the journey.

Allow yourself room for mistakes. Be patient with yourself.
But stay the course with intention.

Focus all your energy on this process.
This is your time. This is your moment.

Let's Get Intentional

Here's your first action step.

Grab a notebook or open your notes app.

Write down everything you're passionate about. Don't filter. Don't judge. Just brainstorm. Spend ample time contemplating your passions. Take a few days if needed. Write down everything and everywhere you find happiness. Those are your passions. Write them all down.

Don't limit yourself. This is a "get to know yourself" project. Let all your ideas be recorded without judgment. Don't attach yourself to the likelihood of whether it is realistic or not. If you love baseball but aren't good enough to play in the big leagues, there is still a place for you in the baseball community. If you love science but don't have a degree in chemical engineering, there is still a place for you in the science community.

Be honest with yourself and allow your passions to be important. There is no wrong answer here. This is about you.

Once you have your list of possible passions to pursue, narrow it down to one direction.

This may seem difficult, but you're not locked in. You can pivot later. The point is to get started. This is the first step. Pick one and let's move to the next step.

On a new page, write the name of your chosen passion. For example: "Scuba Diving." You've now set your intention. It is time to make a plan.

Build a Simple Plan and Find Your Community

Ask yourself two questions:

1. **How can I meet people who share this passion?**
2. **How can I learn more about this passion?**

Using the scuba diving example:

- **Meet people:** Join a scuba club. Attend a diving expo.
- **Learn more:** Take a scuba class. Research scuba gear. Watch YouTube tutorials.

Apply the same logic to your passion. Start small. Write 2–3 actionable steps under each question.

Now, organize those steps in order of ease from simplest to most involved.

And then: take action.

It sounds simple, but these are the necessary steps in your new journey. Take them seriously and you will find that these simple two actions will open more doors and lead to new opportunities. Furthermore, the next steps in your journey will become clear through these experiences.

Get started today.

On Failure and Why You Need It

Now that you have a direction and a plan, let's talk about failure for a moment. This is important to know from the beginning.

You will fail. It's not optional. It's part of the process.
And that's a good thing.
Failure teaches…It refines… It forces you to grow.

In 2001, I started a video game business. After six years of struggling to achieve a profit, I only had one option. I had to change directions. I had to close down my business and move on. It was the toughest decision I have ever made. It came with towering consequences. I thought I had failed my family and myself. I thought that the video game business was such a failure that it meant that I really wasn't cut out to be an entrepreneur. I was sure this failure would define my life and that there wasn't any way to bounce back. I can't really even sum up into words the devastation that I felt during this time.

Come to find out, the reality was that within about 6 months, all of the gloom had washed away. It took time to get things fully back on track, but it wasn't nearly as bad or as long as I had imagined.

But guess what? That experience led me to art. It taught me resilience. And it gave me the strength to succeed in a new field.

That wasn't the failure I thought it was. It was **failing forward**.

Even today, I face setbacks. When Dana and I moved to L.A. in 2017 to expand our business, things were great until the pandemic hit. Then, a fire destroyed our studio. We lost everything to smoke damage.

It was another brutal chapter. But we didn't stop. We adapted. We adjusted. We learned. That's what it means to fail forward.

Champions

As you set on this journey of self-discovery and passion, it will serve you well to seek out one or two (or ten) mentors.

Ideally, these wise souls will have been down the path you are going or something very similar.

You want mentors:

- With extensive experience in a field, ideally the one you are exploring.
- Who will give you constructive feedback in a positive and nurturing way.
- Who will cheer you on when you succeed and help lift you up when you fall.

Finding the right mentor is as easy as the first steps you took. These people will be members of the very local clubs or organizations that you will be joining.

The people who make the best mentors are typically found where philanthropy is involved. The best mentors are already contributing to the betterment of those around them. They are out there waiting for you to ask them for help.

With one or two of the right mentors, you will acquire the tools, the know-how, and the support for your journey.

My current happiness is due in part to my wonderful mentors. I will be forever grateful for their presence in my life.

Time to Act

> **"Inaction breeds doubt and fear. Action breeds confidence and courage."** —Dale Carnegie.

> **"People of accomplishment rarely sat back and let things happen to them. They went out and happened to things."**
> —Leonardo Da Vinci.

> **"To hell with circumstances; I create opportunities."**
> —Bruce Lee

You've set your intention.
You've made your list.
You know what to do.
Now it's time to **take action**.

Start with one goal a day. Use your list as your guide.
When you complete the list, make a new one.

Don't get stuck thinking long-term. Just keep moving.

Track your progress and hold yourself accountable to continuing the process.

The success of your journey will rely largely on the amount of action you take.

The Good Stuff

I am currently in one of the happiest phases of my life.

I have had my share of unhappy and unfulfilled years. And, even now, I still stumble. I still struggle. I still fail. I am not perfect, and my life is not perfect. To be clear, my life can sometimes seem like complete chaos. Pursuing my passion hasn't solved all of my problems.

Pursuing my passion has given me purpose, happiness, and peace. It has provided me with a community of like-minded friends. It has given me confidence in myself. I am truly fulfilled.

I am grateful for my journey, my struggles, my lessons, and my mentors.

I hope that you are inspired to get started, take action, and step into the forest. Just remember…

Be intentional about your journey.
Reset your mindset.
Make a plan.
Embrace failure.

Seek your community.
Seek your champions.
Act. And act again.
Enjoy the process.

Your Passion Is Waiting

This is your moment.
Not next year.
Not when things are "perfect."
Not when you feel more ready.
Now.

You have what it takes.
You don't need permission.
You need to begin.
You need to JUMP!

Your passion is waiting.
Life is waiting.

DAWN NELSON, MSW, CPC

Dawn Nelson is a MSW, a trained Clinical Hypnotherapist and a Certified Professional Coach. She spent 25 years as a psychotherapist in private practice, working with individuals, couples, and families. She has been providing life coaching services since 2006.

Dawn believes in creating lives and businesses by design. She works with individuals to enhance their lives by focusing on behaviors that produce real-life changes supporting growth and development, both personally and professionally. As a coach, Dawn sees her role as one of trainer and motivator, asking clients to do more than they would do on their own. She is a frequent public speaker and facilitates workshops and seminars on a number of topics.

Her current practice focuses exclusively on Coaching. She helps people advance their careers and their businesses, enhance their personal and business relationships, and improve their lives.

Dawn has an extensive history of community involvement. Her passion is helping people create better ways of working, living, and relating to each other.

To learn more about opportunities to work with Dawn, visit: MyCoachDawnNelson.com, or email her at: dawnenelson@hushmail.com.

CHAPTER 17

THE IMAGINATION BLUEPRINT— FROM DREAM TO ENTERPRISE

By Dawn Nelson, MSW, CPC

From the time I was six years old, I knew I wanted to build something of my own. Not just a business but a life designed with intention, fueled by passion, and guided by purpose. My first foray into entrepreneurship was humble but formative: a lawn care service co-founded with a neighborhood friend. He had the mower; I had the drive. Together, we knocked on doors, offered our services, and took pride in every blade of grass we trimmed.

We didn't know it then, but we were laying the foundation for a mindset that would shape our futures. That early experience taught me something essential: entrepreneurship is not about the size of the venture; it's about the spirit behind it. It's about initiative, ownership, and the joy of creating value.

The Spark Reignited

Years later, during a successful career as a psychotherapist, I found myself once again at a crossroads. While attending the Hypnotherapy Academy of America, something shifted. I can't recall the exact moment, but I remember the feeling like a freight train of clarity and conviction. I knew I had to build something new, something that integrated the transformative tools I was learning with my lifelong passion for helping others. This was more than a career pivot. It was a reclamation of a dream and a commitment to live it out loud.

Imagination: The Architect of Reality

Albert Einstein once said, "Imagination is more important than knowledge." I've found this to be profoundly true. Knowledge informs, but imagination ignites. When we activate our imagination with clarity and emotion, we engage the subconscious mind in powerful ways. It begins to work overtime, aligning our thoughts, behaviors, and even our environment to support our vision. But imagination alone isn't enough. A dream without a deadline is just a wish. That's why I teach my clients and live by this principle myself: "An idea without an 'on or before' date is not a goal. It's a fantasy."

The Power of Mentorship

No one builds a dream alone. Throughout my journey, I've been blessed with extraordinary mentors, each one a catalyst for growth that propelled me towards my goals.

> **Douglas Thibodeaux, M.D.,** was an obstetrician/gynecologist who brought birthing rooms to Houston and delivered over 30,000 babies in a long and devoted career. He was the first Chief of Staff at Memorial City Herman Hospital in West Houston. Doug grew up in a French Cajun family with five children, and he didn't speak English until the third grade. He highly prized education and encouraged me to pursue my dreams and earn an undergraduate degree while still managing the business side of a booming veterinary hospital. Despite many challenges during my

pursuit of that degree, he was always there, offering positive words, reassurance, and encouragement. Doug helped me see that with each step I took, I was building a strong and viable future. He modeled stability at a time when I did not have much. In the midst of challenges, Doug had a calm and confident approach. Among those who knew him, he was famous for assessing issues quickly and thoroughly, often saying, "It's not a problem." And he meant it. He was a solution finder who exuded humble confidence. When I wanted to apply to graduate school, Doug inspired me to continue my education and focus on the dream of being a practicing psychotherapist. This ultimately led to a life of meaning, joy, and fulfillment.

Bob Orkin, a visionary shopping center developer, challenged me to leave a secure corporate role in business development and pursue my calling in psychotherapy. He handed me a book that changed my life: Do What You Love, the Money Will Follow by Marsha Sinetar. That book and his belief in me permitted me to leap.

John Bartley, LCSW, my clinical mentor, taught me to focus on my own path, to keep learning, and to prioritize self-care. His advice was simple but profound: "Let go of what others are doing. Stay curious. Stay grounded." With a gift for communicating on a deep and meaningful level with clients, he taught me to understand my audience. He also led by example. When the client came in and the door closed, all energy was totally focused in the moment, speaking in a manner that resonated with them.

Herb Weiss, PhD, a retired chemical engineer and founder of a publicly traded company, became a mentor in my entrepreneurial evolution. He was tech-savvy, sharp, and unrelentingly curious. He pushed me to think bigger, to embrace technology, and to recognize my gift for teaching. Herb asked tough questions that I had not even considered.

As different as each of these mentors was, they had great similarities: they were optimistic and pragmatic, they expected a lot from themselves and others, they were persistent, and they shared the same value system. They all lived lives of service. These mentors didn't just offer advice; they also offered belief. And that belief became fuel.

From Vision to Reality

When I finally committed to launching my own practice, I did so with intention. I visualized the space: serene, nature-infused, welcoming. I imagined the clients I would serve, the breakthroughs they would experience, and the joy I would feel doing work I loved. Within weeks, I found the perfect location ten times the size of my previous space, with rent three times higher. The old version of me might have hesitated. But this time, I was ready. I had a plan, a coach, and a fire in my belly.

Together, we broke the goal into actionable steps. Daily progress. Bite-sized wins. A 90-day launch window. And on the other side of that commitment? A thriving business rooted in purpose.

The Takeaway

Entrepreneurship is not reserved for the lucky or the fearless. It's for the committed. The curious. The ones willing to imagine boldly and act consistently.

So here's your challenge:

Write down your dream. Give it a date. Break it into steps. Ask for help. And then start. Because the life you imagine isn't just possible, it's waiting for you to claim it.

Faith in Motion: The Mindset That Builds Momentum

This time was different. Something had shifted not just in my circumstances, but in my consciousness. My mindset had transformed. I no longer hoped for success; I expected it. My mind had become a goal-striving mechanism, calibrated for clarity, action, and results. I was ambitious. I was eager. And most importantly, I was committed. Each day, I moved with purpose, checking off tasks in sequential order. I wasn't just working, I was building. Exactly three months from the day I set my intention, I watched my vision materialize. While I was seeing clients, my niece was packing up my office for the movers. The date I had written down had become the day my new business was born.

The Breakthroughs That Mattered Most

Early on, one of the most powerful breakthroughs came in the form of a space, a treatment room with a picture window overlooking a lush, green landscape. It was everything I had imagined. The most astonishing part? I had driven past it for years without noticing. The breakthrough was understanding the power of aligned intention: when your mind is clear and your heart is open, what you need often reveals itself right in front of you. Looking back, it was an act of faith paired with focused, purposeful action. I believed good things could happen, and they did.

The Courage to Choose Autonomy

Two early challenges stand out as defining moments in my entrepreneurial journey. The first was telling my mentor I was going out on my own. It wasn't easy. I had deep respect for him; he had opened the door to my professional path. But he responded with grace and encouragement. He knew I loved the work and, unlike many of my peers, genuinely enjoyed the business side of the profession. The second challenge was more radical: I chose to walk away from insurance panels and third-party payors. At the time, this was considered a risky, even reckless, move. Most professionals relied on those systems for a steady stream of clients. But I knew I wanted to practice on my terms. I made a list of pros and cons and chose freedom. I chose to spend my time in meaningful work with clients, not justifying treatment plans to bureaucracies. That decision allowed me to witness something extraordinary: the miracle of healing, unencumbered by red tape. I watched people rise from trauma, reclaim their lives, and step into wholeness.

The Joy of a Purpose-Driven Career

For over 25 years, I've had the privilege of doing work that brings me joy. Every day, I've helped people overcome adversity, tap into their God-given gifts, and build lives of meaning, fulfillment, and peace.

The most valuable financial lesson I've learned. Do what you love, and the money will come. When your work aligns with your purpose, every day becomes a gift. I couldn't wait to get to my office. My work was a laboratory or learning, and my clients were some of my greatest teachers.

Rewiring the Financial Mindset

One of the most profound shifts I experienced was around money. My old mindset was rooted in scarcity: There's not enough. You don't deserve it. It's not good. However, through study, mentorship, and spiritual growth, I developed a different mindset there is more than enough. I want what God wants me to have. I openly receive God's gifts. This shift brought peace, generosity, and a deeper sense of trust in the process.

Marketing with Heart and Strategy

In the early days, I relied on traditional marketing print ads, public speaking, and word of mouth. I focused on women within a 15-mile radius who believed in investing in personal growth. However, I soon discovered that people who truly wanted help would drive much farther. My market expanded organically, driven by opportunity and my passion for teaching. One unexpected breakthrough came from volunteering at a seminar for women going through divorce. That experience opened the door to a new client base: men who wanted to save their marriages. I leaned into this opportunity, drawing on my training with renowned experts like Michele Weiner-Davis and Terry Real. Their work deepened my understanding of relationships and helped me serve this new audience with confidence and compassion.

Lessons from the Field

I'm not sure what made me entrepreneurial. Perhaps it was watching my uncle, one of the few business owners I knew growing up. He seemed to live with freedom, curiosity, and a sense of purpose. I wanted that. I wanted to understand every part of a business and have the freedom to shape my own path. If I could go back, I would have invested more in media and marketing. With a background in mass media and speech, I was comfortable on stage, but I often worked behind the scenes. A media expert could have helped me amplify my message and reach a wider audience.

Still, I have no regrets. The journey has been rich, rewarding, and deeply aligned with my values.

Your Next Steps

Entrepreneurship is not just about building a business. It's about creating a life. A life of purpose, freedom, and contribution. So here's what I encourage you to do:

- Look for opportunities. They're often hiding in plain sight.
- Think positively. Your thoughts are the software that runs your mind.

- Write your goals down with a date. Make them real.
- Break your goals into small, actionable steps. Progress is built one step at a time.
- Ask for help. Mentors, coaches, and community are essential.
- Say yes to growth. Invest in yourself. Share your gifts. Be available.

And above all, believe in your vision, your value, and the possibility of a life you love. It's waiting for you!

Fear Not!

Let fear not be your leader
Let fear not hold your hand
Let fear not be your compass
Let fear not be your band

Fear will never fail you.
Because fear will never try
For fear has all the reasons
To keep you from reaching towards the sky

Fear will give you freedom.
From ridicule, hardships, and pain
Free from failure, abundance, and certainly
Free from fame

Fear lives in the darkness
And won't see the light of day
Fear won't know the future,
nor love, nor glory, nor pay.

—Peter C. Remington

GERARD A. OBRIEN

Gerard is the President, CEO, and Founder of **ORION Ambulance Services**, one of the leading emergency medical service providers in the Greater Houston area. A Boston native who moved to Houston at the age of nine, he earned his Bachelor's Degree in Business and Commerce from the **University of Houston–Downtown**, majoring in Real Estate with a minor in Business Administration.

Gerard began his career as a commercial real estate appraiser, earning the prestigious MAI designation and gaining experience in both private and banking sectors. After a decade in real estate, he transitioned to the utility management industry before launching his entrepreneurial journey in the early 2000s, first in the automobile leasing business and later in healthcare. In 2007, he founded **ORION EMS**, building it from the ground up into a trusted name in emergency medical services known for its commitment to excellence and innovation.

A dynamic leader with a strong analytical foundation, Gerard is skilled in business development, communication, negotiation, and strategic growth. He currently serves on the **Board of Directors of the Texas Ambulance Association** and the **EMS Advisory Council at Houston Community College**, where he continues to champion high standards and progress within the EMS industry.

> "I truly believe that people will support that which they helped build."

Get your team involved in the growth of your company.

CHAPTER 18

PATRON OF PERSISTENCE

By Gerard A. OBrien

At some point in my life, people started referring to me as a serial entrepreneur…and I had to wonder…Fruit Loops or Cocoa Puffs. Then I suddenly realized that they were referring to me as someone who had business successes in different, varied industries. Aha!

I started as an accounting major in school and was so bored that I was distracted by the trappings of living alone away from home. Once I **fell** into the path that I took for a degree, I thrived. After graduation, I went into a commercial real estate appraisal career. There was still the nagging feeling that something was missing; I was not fulfilled. I stumbled through this commercial real estate phase, obtaining the MAI designation in that industry and moving from private companies into the banking arena.

As an entrepreneur, I have started two vehicle leasing companies, an IV therapy spa, and a private ambulance company, and worked for an energy management company throughout my various careers. I have stumbled, succeeded, and failed all along the way. I became the #3 salesperson in the country for radio frequency utility management products, beginning an itch for sales that has not subsided over the years. None of this was ever something I started out to do or planned to begin.

As most, I started school in one field of study and progressed into another by way of twists and turns. All of us can expect, and should welcome, the 'twists and turns of business'. Do not shy away from what presents itself, and certainly stay flexible throughout your business career.

As you progress through your career path, you will meet people who will inspire you, excite you, and promote you and your ideas. These people will become your personal advisors and your mentors. Nurture these relationships, ask their advice, and thank them often for the help they offer you.

One mentor has influenced my life immeasurably and remains a close confidant and good friend. That man is Tony Siress. A success on his own in the tech world, he saw something in me and began to push me to "do my own thing". He started by suggesting books and taught me to focus on the what-ifs of business. Tony remains a close advisor, part of my brain trust, and a great sounding board for concepts and projects that have come up.

Early in my professional career, I remember feeling jealous of friends who ran their own businesses and had this freedom that was so alluring. Freedom. Freedom to set their own schedule. Freedom to work as hard, or not as hard as they saw fit. Ultimately, freedom to live life!

This jealousy led me to seek out entrepreneurial opportunities on my own…a daunting task for sure. Through several mentors, I was able to shape a train of thought that led me to measure and decide what risks were worth taking. And there I was, off and running!!

I must say the term "so what" became one of my mantras…So what? Why does your idea mean something to you? And how will it mean something to the ultimate consumer of your 'product'? It is a very useful phrase to help you weed out the noise and focus on the idea at hand.

One of the most daunting tasks of beginning any business is raising capital. Yikes! However, no pain, no gain. So I adapted and educated myself in learning how to ask people for money, investing in an idea or a dream I had. This became my first and most adept sales skill...and you too must develop this skill.

Family and friends are the most likely source and can be the foundation of seed money for the development of a business concept. The next best route is to develop relationships with bankers. These relationships can be fruitful and turn into advisory sources for all your business needs. I remain very close to one banker who has guided me through the processes of borrowing money and lowering my risk.

Once the monies are secured, it is now time to make the rubber hit the road. Once the concept or idea is born, it has to be nurtured and implemented. How was I to communicate, educate, and indoctrinate these investors into my idea...my world?

Well, once again, sales became the key concept. Selling your widgets, your plan, your vision to someone else can be difficult, but it is key to realizing your dream...your goal. No easy task, but if the idea solves someone else's problem, becomes the solution of a group, or becomes something people need, your job has become nothing more than communication. Definitions and descriptions of your idea become the way to communicate. To communicate your vision...your dream.

Back to my personal experience. My wise Father taught my brothers and sister's and me: Mush on. Setbacks are to be expected...anticipated. No matter what they are, keep going. The second thing he taught us: This too shall pass. Wow, what a nugget of experience and knowledge to pass down to anyone 'trying' to accomplish something!! (THANKS DAD!)

The first vehicle leasing company venture was my first as an entrepreneur. A very naïve entrepreneur. I was a minority owner. Never, NEVER, EVER be this person. Pass on the opportunity if this is the case…you will thank me later. More at the end about this. I came in as an angel investor when the company needed my capital to survive…if only I had known my worth at that time. Nonetheless, off I go and we grow the company by leaps and bounds. As the partnership soured, I was bought out. The richest part of this story is that these 2 partners were dumb enough to buy me out, give me a giant check and forgot to get me to sign a non-compete. Lesson Learned: there are smart people that do dumb things on every corner. Shame on you for not noticing; yea for me for noticing.

Within 6 weeks' time I was figuratively and literally around the corner, with new business partners, setting up shop with a directly competitive business. Did we kill it…heck ya! I did steal employees, but they were not loyal, and the managing partner was an awful man…so no one would have stayed anyway.

We carried on for several months, perhaps even a year-and-a-half or so before my partners came to me and said they thought they could do it better themselves…inviting me to move on…without a buy-out scenario. Offended and wounded, I had no choice but to move on.

Fortunately, at the time, I had another business partner that we were looking for something else to do and an opportunity to enter the private ambulance industry was presenting itself. Talk about living proof of "ignorance is bliss". You're looking at it right here, right now. #trust We knew as much as you probably know about ambulances right now: they're big, red or white, have lights on them and you mooooove out of the way when they come up behind you.

Well, we didn't go to the low dive, we didn't go to the medium dive… we went ALL the way up to the high dive…and jumped. Little did we know at the time (ignorance) that there were over 400 private ambulances services in Houston, Texas. Even worse, Houston, Texas was the epicenter of Medicare fraud in the ambulance industry. However, there we were swimming around in the deep end, amongst the sharks we had no idea existed.

We blindly went about our business, me selling our services to all that needed it. In the beginning it was slow (as it always is), but we suddenly got our stride and off we went. Contract after contract after contract came in. The joke amongst our early employees was, "we'll get to 8-10 ambulances, lift our heads up off the desk and see how it feels". The joke being that none of us remember having only 8-10 ambulances… we were at 12, 15, 18 and BAM!

The trials and tribulations were robust. Growing a business alone, with no "ambulance company manual" was stressful and trying. Not only at the office, but also at home. Know that there are sacrifices to be made along the way…some together with a life partner, and some that may not be supported within a relationship. It is a tough road, but a necessary one. You will be presented with the challenges that must be decided.

My business partner was understanding most of the time…a rarity for sure. We grew and grew and grew…and would anyone like to know why they call it growing pains…CAUSE IT HURTS!! During the growth stage I oversaw hiring, training and keeping the company on the right track. Remember, we knew NOTHING about the private ambulance business and there was no manual to order off Amazon. Hiring was a learning process and eventually I learned certain key words and cues that would come up during the interviews. This was critical to determining whether someone would fit into our culture and become a good team member in our fledgling organization. Lots of hiring…lots of firing.

The training aspect of our process was very simplistic in that if your mother taught you everything you needed to know when you were a young child (comb your hair, tuck your shirt in, buckle your belt, be on time…and above all…be polite) then I had Professional Sr. EMT's that could train you on the equipment and medical standards. If you didn't pay attention to what Mom was trying to teach you at that young tender age, then I could not train you as an adult.

Keeping everyone motivated and adhering to our standards was a large component of our success. The accolades that poured in were a nice reinforcement of our culture and provided motivation to the staff. Inspiration came from noting how our business thrived in an already crowded market. It struck a tone that provided evidence that we were on the right track and doing the right things.

Along the way, the understanding of a business partner really depends on your Yin & Yang. Let me take a moment to expound on this.

YIN & YANG : I'm the salesperson, he was the money guy. Our skills were in different areas, and that really helped. We generally stayed in our own lanes and rarely wandered into each other's specialty. I can say with confidence that it is important to recognize and express gratitude to the partner that handles the tasks you have no expertise in. This is crucial in the long run and should be recognized early and often.

My time and life were consumed. And eventually it paid off. As we grew, we strived, suffered and succeeded. The pattern that everyone will experience and eventually want. To recognize these phases is very key to the acknowledgement you owe yourself. The personal accolades and pats-on-the-back you deserve.

Now, 17 years on, we have over 25 ambulances and a robust staff with all our managers home grown. We have a stellar reputation in the marketplace within an industry full of less than shining stars. The key message we carried with us every day was that we do it for the people. This has communicated our dedication to quality service within the healthcare community and hospital systems.

I'd have to say that what I am most proud of are the successes the team has experienced. They have grown into mature men and women, started families and bought homes. Their career paths have been enriched by their tenure with our company and that is a special success. This is a personal accolade that I give myself, having provided the environment, the culture and the opportunities for them to grow.

For myself, the business has been both challenging and rewarding. It has fulfilled my life with a huge accomplishment, but not without sacrifice. Personal relationships have suffered and potential aspects of my life may have been ignored or even missed. I have no regrets and do not dwell on the woulda-shoulda-coulda things that crop up in my mind every now and again. The business has provided so many achievements that it would be hard to assess where failures or regrets could be measured and quantified as material shortcomings.

The passion I have developed for the ambulance Industry is deeply rooted in my involvement in the tight knit community that makes up the industry. The gratitude of helping others proves that we come to work every day to serve the people. The patients. The hospital staff. The emergency room staff. And of course, the employees. I am a past President of the Texas Ambulance Association and remain an active Board Member, keeping a keen eye on the industry to promote best practices. The interaction with fellow owners, industry vendors and participants throughout the EMS field is a gratifying motivator.

Our company continues to support local charities and area leaders to provide outreach and support for the local citizens. Helping non-profit organizations in their efforts to help less fortunate individuals is a key component of our business plan. All companies should do what they can to support the efforts of these groups.

MICKEY O'NEAL

Mickey O'Neal, CPA, is an entrepreneur, author, and trusted financial advisor who leads **ONealCPA PLLC**, a boutique accounting firm dedicated to helping small business owners build lasting financial success. With a personalized, white-glove approach, Mickey guides entrepreneurs toward sustainable growth, independence, and long-term stability.

Specializing in income tax planning for high-net-worth individuals and small to midsize businesses, he serves clients across industries including healthcare, construction, and energy. His passion lies in supporting the small business community, the true backbone of the U.S. economy, by helping owners avoid costly mistakes and achieve their goals with confidence.

A seasoned advisor, Mickey has guided companies through remarkable growth, including a healthcare startup that achieved a $100 million private equity exit under his financial leadership. He has written for Texas Monthly and numerous industry journals and co-authored *Chart of Accounts for Healthcare Organizations* for the **Center for Research in Ambulatory Healthcare Administration**.

Before founding ONealCPA PLLC, Mickey was the managing partner of two successful CPA firms. Beyond business, he is a devoted husband, father, and grandfather who enjoys golf, racquetball, and giving back through organizations such as the **Houston Downtown Rotary, Visage Worldwide, and Whiteboards N Whiskey.**

ONealCPA.net

CHAPTER 19

A LIFE BUILT ON NUMBERS: ENTREPRENEURS TURN VISION INTO VALUE AND VALUE INTO EQUITY

By Mickey O'Neal

O**NealCPA PLLC was** created in July 2021 and began operations two months later. This timeline is significant. We were emerging from the Coronavirus pandemic, a period that didn't just disrupt the economy but also reshaped the entire landscape of how we work, live, and interact.

That timing wasn't accidental. It was a statement. We chose to build something new when the world was still uncertain. That's the heart of entrepreneurship: building through fog. This chapter captures a slice of that journey. It's not the whole story, far from it. There are references like "more on that later" for a reason: I'm writing a second book to explore those deeper layers fully. Consider this a glimpse into a life of reinvention, challenge, and service one that continues to unfold.

This is the third CPA firm I've founded from scratch. But as with every major venture in my life, I didn't do it alone. Entrepreneurship is never a solo endeavor; it's a relay race, a tag-team, a chorus of mentors, partners, and supporters who show up at just the right time. In the past, I built firms alongside other CPAs. Some were brilliant. Some, not so much. Some had integrity. Others... less so. These partnerships taught me hard lessons about trust, alignment, and the cost of compromise. When I launched ONealCPA, I did so post-pandemic, while navigating litigation and negative working capital. But this time, I had a different kind of team.

The women in my life became my foundation.

Strength in Community, Strength in Family

My wife, Hisae O'Neal, supported me in every way, emotionally, spiritually, and financially. She coined the phrase "Make Mickey Great Again," and while it started as a rallying cry, it quickly became a guiding principle. She believed in me when I wasn't sure I believed in myself. Being Japanese, she also encouraged me to rely more on family and less on others, which is the Japanese way. She was right, and I listened.

Brenda Cheney, whom I first hired in the early 1990s as a marketing professional, has been another constant. She's one of those rare talents who, when placed in the proper role, becomes transformative. Brenda has now led marketing at two of my firms. Her instincts, energy, and strategic thinking have helped define our brand and connect us to our community in authentic ways. That philosophy extends to my own family. In recent years, I've had the great honor of introducing my daughter, Natalie, to the tax profession and to ONEALCPA. Watching her grow into her role, develop her voice, and carry the values of service and integrity forward has been one of the most rewarding experiences of my life. I didn't just want to teach Natalie how to prepare taxes, I wanted to show her how to build relationships, solve problems, and serve with her heart. She's doing all of that and more. She joined our team in 2023 as a tax professional and has quickly become one of the most proactive members. Her approach is fresh, thoughtful, and fearless. Watching her grow has been one of the most profound joys of my professional life. Her entry into the firm marked a turning point; it wasn't just a business anymore. It was a legacy.

A Foundation of Independence

I grew up in Pasadena, Texas, as the third child of two scientists. My father was with Shell Oil for over four decades as a physicist. My mother, a chemist, left Humble Oil (now Exxon) to raise us. A baby boomer born to a middle-class family, we lived a middle-class life filled with discipline, curiosity, and expectation.

As the youngest, I had to find my own voice early. That independence equal parts necessity and personality shaped me profoundly. I've failed plenty of times. Some of those failures were public. Others were quietly devastating. But I've always rebounded. Each setback refined me. Sharpened my vision. Strengthened my resolve.

From these experiences, I formed the four core values that now anchor ONEALCPA:

- **Honesty**: Speak the truth, even when it's hard.
- **Serving Others**: Prioritize relationships over transactions.
- **Striving for Excellence**: Always raise the bar.
- **Openness to Change**: Evolve or become irrelevant.

These values are more than slogans. They're filters. Every decision we make passes through them.

From Numbers to Narrative

I earned my degree from the University of Houston Business Administration with a focus in accounting. I was drawn to the precision of numbers, but more so to their potential. Numbers tell stories. They reveal patterns. They expose weaknesses and illuminate strengths. They are tools for clarity in chaos.

Early in my career, I worked at Brown & Root and Coopers & Lybrand, both the largest in the world in their respective industries. Those environments were rigid, hierarchical, and stifling. I quickly realized I wasn't built for bureaucracy. I was built for risk, for creativity, for building. So, I started my own firm. I was a one-man band with a Compaq "portable" computer and a vision. Within a few years, that vision scaled into one of the top 25 CPA firms in Houston, as recognized by the Houston Business Journal. I had no blueprint, just grit and trust in people.

Building a Business With Soul

When I launched O'Neal McGuinness & Tinsley, it wasn't just about building a client base it was about creating a philosophy of leadership. I believed in leading with character, not charisma. I believed clients were not line items, but long-term partners. I believed a team should be developed, not just managed.

That belief was tested and refined when I served as an SEC audit partner with Malone & Bailey. I worked with publicly traded companies, navigating complex financial landscapes, intense scrutiny, and relentless pressure. It taught me to lead under fire and never compromise on ethics.

Later, I built Thayer O'Neal PLLC, scaling it to over 40 employees and $4 million in annual revenue. That growth was a result of mindset, not marketing. We showed up for clients…We educated…We listened. And we always looked out for our team. An employee once said at an event, she felt like it was more a family than a business.

Mentorship: The Legacy That Matters Most

If there is a throughline to everything I've done, it's mentoring. Whether I was working with a medical group navigating a merger or a young CPA trying to understand a complex audit engagement, I saw every interaction as an opportunity to teach, uplift, and develop character.

I'm proud of the number of young professionals who have come through my firms and gone on to lead their practices or take on executive roles elsewhere. Some were interns who didn't yet know what a journal entry was. Others were experienced hires burned out by the "big firm" grind. I gave them space to grow and pushed them when they needed it.

Mentorship, to me, isn't about handholding. It's about truth-telling with compassion. It's about seeing potential in someone before they see it themselves. It's about holding them to a higher standard than they think they can reach, and then walking beside them until they do.

Entrepreneurial Lessons from the Field

Throughout my career, I've worked with entrepreneurs in many industries. Each sector has its nuances, but the core entrepreneurial traits are universal: tenacity, resilience, curiosity, decisiveness, and the ability to manage uncertainty.

Through my position as a trusted advisor, I've had a front-row seat to the decision-making process of some of Houston's most dynamic leaders. I've seen what works and what doesn't.

An example is a long-term acute care hospital system for which I was the tax advisor chair of the audit committee of the board of directors. Starting with seed capital of about $600 thousand in 2004, it sold through a private equity offering in 2009 for over $100 million.

One lesson that sticks with me is this: Cash flow is king, but mindset rules. I've watched companies with solid finances crumble because the leadership lacked vision or integrity or simply because of changes in economic conditions.

Members of this hospital system created a specialty surgical hospital chain across Texas. Growing to over $60 million in revenue, spinning off $20 million in dividends in only a few years. The Company went bankrupt when Obamacare forced providers into managed networks.

What separates successful entrepreneurs from the rest is not just their financial literacy, it's leadership. Their ability to communicate, delegate, and pivot when hard times arise, which they inevitably will and to make tough decisions without losing their humanity. Those are the traits I aim to cultivate in my team and in every business owner I work with.

Leadership by Intention

Leadership, like accounting, is both art and science. You need technical expertise, sure. But you also need empathy, timing, and the courage to act.

I lead by example. Whether it's showing up early, staying late, or admitting a mistake, I do not ask my team to do anything I would not do myself. That consistency builds trust, and trust builds high-performing teams.

Consensus-building is also critical in managing a professional services firm. I take pride in working through consensus-building. I have always sought to lead by creating agreement on direction.

One of my favorite ways to lead is through stories. I'll often share real client scenarios to help young accountants understand the impact of their work. When they realize they're not just entering numbers but shaping the financial health of a company, they step up in powerful ways.

Value demonstration through storytelling is also essential. Public accounting has undergone a significant transformation due to technology. That change continues with the advent of Artificial Intelligence. Pivoting away from hourly billing to value billing has become a necessity as we eliminate the mundane, repetitive, and costly routines with efficient processes.

Networks That Shape Leaders

Leadership isn't a solo sport. You need people around you who challenge you, support you, and expand your perspective. I have been deeply involved in networking and leadership groups throughout my career.

Rotary International has been a source of inspiration and focus for community service. A member of three different clubs, an officer in two and President of one, Rotary has provided me with an avenue to remain grounded in the community while staying connected to a diverse range of leaders and causes.

The Vistage CEO network is a peer advisory group for trusted advisors, CEOs, and business owners. I have been a member of it off and on since 1997. Vistage has sharpened my decision-making and held me accountable to the highest standards of leadership. These groups have helped me grow not just as a business owner but as a person, and they've reinforced the power of community, relationship building, collaboration, and lifelong learning.

Connection as Strategy: Cigar Talk & Beyond

Out of a love for conversation and community, I launched **Cigar Talk**, a networking forum disguised as a hangout. What began as a casual way to unwind with a few business peers became one of the best networking platforms in Houston. Entrepreneurs from all industries come together, share ideas, swap stories, and challenge each other.

We discussed business, but also touched on life, marriage, children, stress, and legacy. There's something about the informal environment that makes people open up. I've watched deals get made, partnerships formed, and lifelong mentorships begin around that circle.

I resurrected the Houston Entrepreneurs Forum, which died in the Pandemic. HEF is a more structured monthly event where a local entrepreneur engages with the audience about his story. It's not a pitch-fest. It's a community. And it reflects the best of what entrepreneurship can help people build a better business and a better life

Giving With Purpose

At ONEALCPA, giving back isn't an initiative; it's who we are. At ONEALCPA, we believe in giving back with intention and consistency. Our annual **Darn to Dream Golf Tournament**, started in 2015 by Thayer O'Neal. 2025 marks our tenth year of benefiting the Leukemia & Lymphoma Society. We don't just raise money, we raise hope.

It's more than just a fundraiser. It's a celebration of hope, resilience, and the power of collective generosity. Every swing of the club brings us closer to funding research, supporting patients, and honoring those who have battled these diseases.

And we're not stopping there. Our next significant initiative is launching a college sponsorship program for aspiring entrepreneurs. I want to help fund the dreams of students who have the heart, the hustle, and the potential, but not the resources, ensuring that talent and heart, not privilege, decide who gets a seat at the table.

Integrity: The Foundation of It All

In every deal, every engagement, every conversation I've held to one core principle: **Do the right thing. Always.** I've turned down business, fired clients, and walked away from lucrative opportunities when they didn't align with our values. Because trust isn't a strategy, it's a sacred responsibility.

When clients trust you with their finances, their taxes, and their strategy, that's sacred. You don't betray that for a dollar or a deal. You guard it with your name, your firm, and your reputation.

Character matters.

Looking Back and Looking Ahead: A Future Worth Building

But I'm not done yet. My vision for ONEALCPA is to continue growing as a firm of integrity-driven advisors, where young accountants come not just to work, but to become leaders. Where clients don't just get returns prepared, but get futures clarified.

People often ask me what I will do when I retire, the answer is produce less and create more. This is my first step, I'm writing more these days, speaking more, investing more in the next generation. I have been recognized on the front page of the business section of the Houston Chronicle. I have written for Texas Monthly and trade publications and co-authored the Chart of Accounts for Healthcare Organizations, published by the Center for Research in Ambulatory Healthcare Administration (the research arm of MGMA). I want to pass along what I've learned not just about accounting, but about resilience, relationships, and reinvention.

Final Thoughts for the Next Generation

If you are a young entrepreneur or aspiring CPA reading this, the five keys to success are simple:

1. **Know Your Numbers**: Whether you're running a business or managing a team, understanding financials is foundational. It's not optional.

2. **Lead with Integrity**: Your reputation is your most valuable asset. Protect it at all costs.
3. **Find a Mentor:** No one succeeds alone. Learn from someone who's walked the path before you.
4. **Be a Lifelong Learner**: The moment you think you've "arrived," you've started to decline. Stay curious.
5. **Serve Others**: Business is not just about profits, it's about people. Serve your clients, your team, and your community well, and success will follow.
6. **Watch Your Back**: Someone is always trying to steal your thunder and ride on your success.

I never set out to be just an accountant. I set out to make an impact. And I've learned that the greatest impact does not come from the technical aspects, it comes from the people you empower along the way.

This is my story. A life led by numbers but defined by people. Would I change it if I could? Absolutely. Although a success, it has in no way been perfect. I've made mistakes and learned along the way and in the words of Rod Stewart:

I wish that I knew what I know now when I was younger.

You have dreams,
and they are easy to see in the stillness of the night
or in the peace of your home.
But during the day, with the hustle and bustle of life,
dreams seem to disappear,
lost in the chaos of the daily noise.
Know this: your dreams are real.
You wouldn't have them if they couldn't become real.
Take time each day to connect with your dreams.
They are right there in front of you,
through the noise.

HELEN PERRY

Helen Perry has built a distinguished career helping individuals and organizations present their best selves, both professionally and personally. Known as a "one-woman Swiss Army knife," she founded her consulting practice in 1983 and quickly became one of Houston's most respected experts in image, communication, and professional development. With her signature mix of wit, warmth, and precision, Perry has guided clients such as **ExxonMobil, Deloitte, BP, and Tiffany & Co.** toward greater confidence and effectiveness.

Through her **P.A.T.H. Program (Professional Awareness Training Heights)**, Perry delivers seminars on impression management, business etiquette, communication, and goal achievement, helping teams from Houston to Mumbai enhance professionalism and presence. Her programs consistently lead to improved morale, stronger communication, and greater productivity.

A three-time recipient of the **Better Business Bureau Pinnacle Award** and named one of **Houston's 50 Most Influential Women**, Perry is also deeply committed to community service. She has volunteered with organizations such as the **Salvation Army, United Way, and Ronald McDonald House**, and created **Eticool School**, teaching manners and character development to more than twelve thousand children.

A woman of faith, humor, and resilience, Perry credits her family, friends, and late sister, Marilyn Sage, for her strength. She and her husband, Doug Simpkins, live in Texas, along with three sons, daughters-in-law, and seven grandchildren.

> "I will get ready and then perhaps my chance will appear."
> –Abraham Lincoln.

Helen-Perry.com

CHAPTER 20

IMPRESSION MANAGEMENT

by Helen Sage Perry

Welcome to the world of entrepreneurship! If you have that passion, that fire in the belly that drives you to make your business work against all odds, you're on the right track. That said, be cognizant of balance, self-care and stress management. This information is sincerely intended to **ease your frustrations, minimize mistakes, and boost your success**. Practicing these easy habits will hasten your path far more efficiently than dismissing them. Undoubtedly, the reason I can teach it is that I've made just about every mistake mentioned! Enjoy…

In our competitive business landscape, first impressions are more critical than ever. Studies suggest that individuals form judgments about others within the first **seven seconds** of an encounter. This rapid assessment underscores the importance of managing one's appearance, behavior, and communication effectively.

Impressions people form depend **more on our behavior than our true personality**. Anyone's perception is their reality. However, there are valid techniques to help us clarify our true intentions. *Impression Management* **is a process by which people might**

alter the perceptions others hold of them. A symbolic interaction theorist, **Erving Goffman**, coined the term Impression Management in 1959 and from then on, sociologists and theorists have been adding insight and importance to the concept. When used ethically, to enrich relationships with an other-centered attitude, IM is invaluable!

While we never have a second chance to make a first impression, there may be some solutions for turning things around if you are dissatisfied with the way others perceive you.

Types of Impression Management:

1. **Authentic**-Used when individual desires to present himself the way he sees himself.
2. **Ideal**-Used to present one's best assets clearly and concisely, allowing others to view him/her most positively. Image makeovers fall into this category, authentically refining dress, speech, online communication, comportment, marketing materials and environment.
3. **Tactical**-Used when an individual desires to present the most popular image in a way the public will perceive him (example: political "spin").

All methods involve sending certain messages to the subconscious mind of people by adapting personal appearance or body language, as well as sending messages to their conscious mind by choosing certain words or actions.

According to nonverbal communication expert Albert Mehrabian, communication consists of 55% appearance, 38% tone of voice and 7% words. Unfair but true, within seconds of meeting someone new, they make at least eleven judgements about us including our trustworthiness, moral character, and future potential. It pays to be objective about ourselves vs. unaware. Note the four levels of consciousness;

1. You don't know you don't know
2. You know you don't know.
3. You know you know.
4. You don't know you know-- highest form of consciousness: intuitive

The way our brains function when we form impressions is complex. Noted Psychologist, the late Dr. Robert Weinberger said, *"All four lobes join forces to contribute in generating signals through our senses. The occipital contributes its visual cues, the temporal stored memories, the frontal past and ongoing experiences and the parietal integration of them all. And even these do not take into account the almost reptilian olfactory forces that are difficult to qualify, yet instinctively and powerfully guide our first impressions without thought. Who among us has not formed an immediate impression based on a foul odor or the sensual allure of Shalimar? The substrates of first impressions, even among the youngest and most naïve human creatures are wonders of neural achievement."*

We move in a fast-paced world. Few get to see the accolades and diplomas on our walls or the philanthropic work we do in our community. Consider Malcolm Gladwell's *Blink:* The main subject of his book is "thin-slicing": Our ability to gauge what is really important from a very narrow period of experience. Spontaneous decisions are often as good as, or even better than, carefully planned and considered ones. Gladwell gives examples of thin-slicing in contexts such as gambling, speed dating, tennis, military war games, malpractice suits, and even predicting divorce.

Your **environment** also speaks volumes. If your office, storefront, clinic, etc. does not appear updated, impressions formed, rightly or wrongly, may be that your goods and services are outdated and possibly inferior.

Objectively assess your image and brand. *Image* changes with trends and style. **Branding** represents the values of a business, the lasting impression or legacy important to its mission. Elements of each are intrinsic to the other. Both must be clear, consistent, and current.

Appearance is the visual gateway to professional success. Crucial behaviors in building your image and brand include dressing as well as you can possibly afford. High-end clothing can be found in resale shops and outlets. Align your attire with the industry culture. A good tailor is a must.

According to The Wall Street Journal (2-22-16), in 2014, assistant professor of organizational behavior at the Yale School of Management, Michael W. Kraus co-authored a study of 128 men ages 18 to 32 with diverse backgrounds and income levels. Results published in the Journal of Experimental Psychology show that clothing with high social status can increase job performance and dominance in "high stakes" competitive tasks. WSJ also notes that in a 2015 study published in the journal Social Psychological and Personality Science, results suggested that people engage in higher levels of abstract thinking when they dress up, compared with when they dress casually.

Good grooming and hygiene aren't optional: They're foundational. Clean, well-kept hair, nails and attire speak volumes about your attention to detail and respect for your work. For women, investing in professional makeup instruction can be a game-changer. Think subtle, strategic, and smart.

Don't underestimate the power of a warm smile with a firm handshake and eye contact. This will put people at ease and make you more approachable. Keep about three feet of distance, never hovering too close. Be gracious, positive, and generous. Express gratitude. Give back to others and to your community. Offer rich content and compelling status updates in your social media posts. Make email messages grammatically correct using simple 10-12 pt. font in blue or black. A complete signature with contact info is essential. Return correspondence promptly via the same medium (texts with text, calls with call, etc.). Keep appointments. Punctuality is a must. Keep your word. Stop behaviors that may be annoying such as loud talking, smacking, self-promoting, interrupting, etc.

Body Language

Without uttering a word, our body language speaks volumes. The physical gestures we make are subconsciously interpreted by others. Some gestures project a very <u>positive message</u>, while others may set a negative tone.

Most people are totally <u>oblivious to their own body language</u>, so the discipline of controlling these gestures can be challenging. Most of them are reflexive in nature, automatically matching up to what our minds are thinking at any given moment. Nevertheless, with the right information and a little practice, we can train ourselves to overcome most of our negative body language habits.

According to Marc Chernoff, the following gestures evoke a negative impression and are ones to eliminate:

1. **Checking the Time or Inspecting Your Fingernails** – strong signs of boredom.
2. **Picking Lint Off of Your Clothes** – especially in conjunction with looking downwards, most people will assume that you disapprove of their ideas.
3. **Stroking Your Chin While Looking at Someone** – "I'm judging you!"
4. **Narrowing Your Eyes--** immediately places a scowling expression on your face.

5. **Looking Down While in the Presence of Others** – usually indicates disinterest and sometimes arrogance. Always look straight ahead and make eye contact.

6. **Touching Your Face During a Conversation** – Face touching, especially on the nose, is commonly interpreted as an indication of deception. Also, covering up the mouth is a common gesture people make when they're lying. Always keep your **hands away from your face** when speaking.

7. **Faking a Smile** – another sign of deception commonly seen on the face of a fraud. A genuine smile wrinkles the corners of the eyes and changes the expression of the entire face. Fake smiles only involve the mouth and lips. It's easy to distinguish between the two.

8. **Leaning Away from Someone** – a sign of being bored and disinterested. Some people may also interpret it to mean: "I don't like you." People typically lean towards people they like and away from people they dislike.

9. **Resting Hands Behind the Head or on the Hips** – usually interpreted as a sign of superiority or bigheadedness.

10. **Standing with Your Hands Crossed Over Your Lower Body** – almost guarantees that you'll lose a little respect before you even have the chance to speak a single word. This guarded stance can appear defensive and uncertain, making your entire body look smaller and weaker.

11. **Crossing Your Arms** – a sign of defensive resistance that may be interpreted as a sign of egotism. Keep your arms open and at your sides.

12. **Displaying a Sluggish Posture** – When you're in an environment bustling with people your posture becomes an immediate sign of your confidence and composure. Place your

feet a comfortable distance apart, keep shoulders pulled back, head up.

13. **Scratching at the Backside of Your Head and Neck** – a typical sign of doubt and uncertainty, sometimes interpreted as an indication of lying.

14. **Increasing Your Rate of Blinking** – a clear sign of anxiety. Some people start blinking their eyes fast (in conjunction with an increased heart rate) when nervous.

15. **Slouching Your Shoulders** – indicates low self-esteem. People associate perked-up shoulders with strong self-confidence.

16. **Propping Up Your Head with Your Hands** – "I'm getting bored!" Never prop up your head with your elbows and hands during a conversation.

17. **Sitting on the Edge of Your Chair** – apprehensive stance that makes others around you feel uncomfortable; a clear indication of being mentally and physically uncomfortable

18. **Foot and Finger Tapping** – usually indicates stress, impatience, or boredom. No fidgeting.

19. **Shifting Body Weight from Foot to Foot** – indicates mental and physical discomfort. People may also assume that you're ready to abandon the conversation.

Communication: The Cornerstone of Effective Leadership

Diaphragmatic vs. shallow breathing will make your tone of voice **appealing and resonant**. Think of the last time you heard someone speak with a flat, dull, or strident voice. Pay attention to articulation and diction without sounding stiff. Use inflection and melody, changing your tone every 3-4 words. Diplomatic, concise word choice is vital: Say what you mean… Mean what you say… But don't say it mean! Avoid unsolicited advice. Focus on saying the right words at the right time in the right way.

Relationships

Research by Gamma in 2024 reveals the tactics successful businesses are using to stay ahead. There is a strong correlation between strong business relationships and commercial success. Businesses prioritizing culture are more likely to see revenue increase. Businesses reporting growth in revenue overperformed on factors including effective problem resolution (74%), good personal relationships with clients (69%) and providing valuable success (68%).

Etiquette

Far more than how you use a fish knife, etiquette is about the way we treat one another, how we maintain relationships. You may have the finest education, the most beautiful home, the greatest athletic talents but **if you do not have good manners**, you will not have as many friends, be invited places, hired for jobs, or accepted to schools. There is one way and one way only to cut your food. Navigating a business lunch or dinner with ease needs to be second nature.

Bad manners over the internet can cause long lasting damage to your reputation. Remember: **Digital = PERMANENT.** Once it's out there, you can never get it back.

When you use good manners to respond to rudeness...

- You stand the best chance of stopping the behavior.
- You stand the best chance of getting what you want.
- You stand the best chance of winning others over to your cause.
- You make the statement that people can't walk over you.
- You maintain your own dignity.
- You set an example that may change the behavior of others.

Be an Influencer

According to John Turner, SeedProd LLC, there are specific traits of influencers. When asked about the most influential people in their life and what set them apart, members of the Young Entrepreneur Council listed the following characteristics they've looked for and identified in their role models:

1. **Help others succeed**

   We often think influential individuals are those we gravitate to, but it's the opposite. Truly influential people train, empower, and create businesses that can operate and run without them, they help gravitate energy *out* instead of toward themselves. Jason Khoo, Zupo

2. **Charismatic**

   The most influential people **light up the room** and **command respect** from people the moment they walk in. One thing that sets them apart is their tendency to not follow the conventional norms, which can be seen in their body language, tonality and presence. Kelly Richardson, Infobrandz

3. **World-class communicators**

   "While styles and methods may differ, those able to effectively master the arts of mass communication and personal persuasion are the most influential individuals in society.", Adam Mendler, The Veloz Group

4. **Confident**

   "The people I admire most are the ones who take bold steps in achieving what the vast majority of the world thinks is unattainable." Jacob Tanur, Click Play Films

5. **Contributors**

    "The most influential people I know have done something that contributes to the world and solves a specific problem. They add undeniable value." Rachel Beider, PRESS Modern Massage

6. **Humility**

    "I find influential people to be very aware of those who helped them become who they are. They're quick to offer praise and credit." Josh Kohlbach, Wholesale Suite

7. **Great listeners**

    "I've always been thankful to have people in my life who are willing to listen. When taking time to listen, true leaders can then understand and provide the best decisions, feedback and advice." Jason Duff, SMALL NATION

8. **Adaptable**

    Influential people can seamlessly reposition the way they think when things don't go according to plan. They are nimble.

Find your **genius zone!** Choose a career that enables you to do things you love so much, you'd do it for free if you didn't have bills to pay! Pay attention to the reactions you receive. If one person tells you you're overbearing or difficult, that's probably their issue. If this type of feedback comes up repeatedly, it's something to assess. A professional consultant can be pivotal in unlocking answers, tweaking behavior, and restoring comfort level in our own skin. This is an **ongoing process** which ultimately leads us to achieve peak performance in our service to others. Embrace these skills and you will enjoy your career finding great fulfillment and peace of mind, knowing you are authentically **being** your best self. **Endeavor to consistently show up with your A-game, let your light shine, pray for guidance and *To thine own self be true.***

Recommended Reading

Contemporary Etiquette
Helen Perry
Book.helen-perry.com/home

The Effective Manager
Mark Horstman

Executive Presence
Sylvia Ann Hewlett

Unreasonable Hospitality
Will Guidara

Power Etiquette-What You Don't Know Can Kill Your Career
Dana May Casperson

The Four Agreements
Don Miguel Ruiz

THERESA ROEMER

Theresa Roemer is an entrepreneur, philanthropist, and luxury lifestyle influencer whose global brand blends elegance, resilience, and purpose. With a career spanning fashion, real estate, fitness, and personal development, Roemer has inspired audiences worldwide to transform their setbacks into comebacks.

Best known for her iconic luxury closet; recognized as the world's largest, Roemer captivates more than 1.5 million followers on Instagram and a growing YouTube community with her motivational content, lifestyle insights, and unfiltered authenticity. As founder of Next Level, an exclusive coaching platform, she leads transformational conversations on business, mindset, and purpose through her popular **Motivational Mondays** series.

Roemer is also the creator and host of **Fashion Woodlands**, a red-carpet charity gala benefiting **Make-A-Wish Texas Gulf Coast and Louisiana**, which celebrated its tenth anniversary. With more than twenty years of experience in luxury real estate, she has built a reputation for excellence in home design, renovation, and entrepreneurial mentorship.

Featured in **Forbes, Harper's Bazaar**, and on national television programs including *Good Morning America, Access Hollywood,* and *The Today Show,* Roemer continues to expand her influence. Originally from Nebraska, she now resides in The Woodlands, Texas, where she is a devoted wife, mother, grandmother, and advocate for grief recovery and personal growth.

> "Success isn't about being seen. It's about being remembered for how you made others rise too."
> – *Theresa Roemer*

TheresaRoemer.com
Instagram.com/theresa.roemer
YouTube: Theresa Roemer

CHAPTER 21

UNAPOLOGETIC, UNBREAKABLE, UNSTOPPABLE

By Theresa Roemer

I often get asked, "Theresa, how did you get here?"

People see the life I live now, the luxury, the closet, the events, the success, but so few understand the road that brought me here. If you really want to know, let me tell you the truth. Not the Instagram version, not the glossy highlight reel , but the raw, imperfect, often painful journey that shaped me into who I am today.

I didn't come from privilege. I wasn't born into a family with connections, wealth, or shortcuts. I was raised on a farm in Nebraska, surrounded by dirt roads, cows, long days of labor, and expectations that left no room for laziness or excuses. On that farm, work wasn't optional, it was survival. If you wanted something, you earned it, with your own two hands, your own grit, your own perseverance.

That mindset, that "get up, push forward" mentality, settled into my bones long before I understood how much it would shape every chapter of my life.

It didn't matter whether I was fighting rheumatic fever , not once, but four times , or living with the weight of a heart murmur. It didn't matter if I was grieving the devastating, unexpected loss of my brother at age 23 or standing knee-deep in a flooded health club I had poured my heart and savings into, watching it all slip away. Even the soul-shattering, unimaginable death of my son or the aching loss of my father couldn't break me completely.

Did those moments bring me to my knees? Absolutely. They crushed me. They forced me to crumble, to fall apart, to cry on the floor in the dark when no one was watching. But each heartbreak, each brutal, gut-wrenching moment, taught me something I carry with me to this day: to rise.

To rise doesn't mean you leap up gracefully. It doesn't mean you're fearless or unbreakable. Rising sometimes means crawling, inch by painful inch, toward a future you can't even picture yet. It means lifting your eyes just enough to remind yourself that you were made for more. That even when the path ahead is covered in pain, it's *your* path, and it's still worth walking.

I think often about the early lessons that shaped me. I remember one summer as a young girl, too sick to help milk the cows. I begged my mother, pleading to let me stay inside just that once. I was burning with fever, weak, dizzy, miserable. But she looked me straight in the eyes and said, **"No."** So I went out, called the cows, sat on the stool, sweating and shaking, throwing up between tasks, tears streaming down my face, silently cursing her in my head. But what I didn't know then, what I only understand now, was that she was teaching me one of the most valuable lessons of my life: Your job, your responsibility, your commitments, they don't disappear just because you're uncomfortable.

Later, after we moved to the city, I got a newspaper route. One winter morning, two feet of snow blanketed the streets. I told my mom I couldn't possibly ride my bike, that it was impossible, that I needed her help. Again, she said, **"No. I didn't sign up for this job, you did. Figure it out."**

I was angry, frustrated. But looking back, I can see it clearly now, I was being shaped. My resilience, my resourcefulness, my work ethic, they were all being forged in those cold, uncomfortable moments when quitting would have been easier but pushing through built strength.

Texas didn't become my home until much later in life, but when I arrived, I knew deep down I was meant to be here. Texas, with its big skies, bold spirit, and wide-open dreams, mirrored everything I had always believed about life. If you're going to dream, dream big. If you're going to show up, show up fully. If you're going to build, build boldly.

What I didn't know then was that Texas would also bring its own lessons. Like when I partnered in business with someone who was also my best friend, only to have the business, and the friendship, fall apart. It left me no alternative but to reinvent myself yet again, to stand up and rebuild, to craft a new path forward. That reinvention helped get me to where I stand today.

People know me now for the glamorous things, the closet, the cars, the handbags, the events. My 3,000-square-foot, three-story closet became a media sensation. At first, I laughed when people fixated on it. **"Really? The closet?"** But I understood. People love a window into a world they think is untouchable, effortless, perfect.

But here's the truth: that closet, filled with decades of fashion and achievement, is just a symbol, it's not the story.

The real story is the woman who fought, scraped, hustled, and bled for every inch of that life.

I have spent my life refusing to let circumstances define me. I've stood on the rooftop of Mount Kilimanjaro, nearly 20,000 feet up in the African sky, not just for the adventure, but because I wanted to prove something to myself, to challenge myself, to remind myself that I could do hard things. I've walked through remote villages where people lacked even the most basic human need, clean, safe water, and I've worked to bring it to them.

But it hasn't just been the wins that shaped me.

I know what it feels like to stand in the rubble of your life, feeling broken beyond repair. I know what it's like to lose a child, to carry a pain so deep, so sharp, that there are no words for it. I know what it's like to fall to the floor, sobbing, wondering how you'll ever stand again.

And still, I rose.

Not because I was fearless. Not because I was invincible. But because I knew I had two choices: stay in the pain or honor the pain by continuing to live, to love, and to lead.

That's the truth no one tells you about success. It's not built only on talent or luck or timing. It's built on heartbreak, on resilience, on a relentless refusal to stay down when life knocks you flat.

That's why I created **Next Level**, my private coaching community where I mentor people who are ready to build their own extraordinary lives. Inside Next Level, we strip away the perfection, the filters, the polished masks. We get real. We do the deep, uncomfortable work. We hold each other accountable. We push, we encourage, we stretch, we grow, together.

Because success means nothing if you're standing alone at the top.

Giving back isn't an afterthought for me; it's at the core of everything I do. That's why every year, I open my home for **Fashion Woodlands**, yes, it's a glamorous event, filled with renowned designers, celebrities, media, and dazzling fashion. But at its heart, it's about purpose.

Each year, we raise funds for **Make-A-Wish Texas Gulf Coast and Louisiana**, an organization deeply meaningful to me. Helping grant life-changing wishes for children facing unimaginable challenges, that's why I do it. That's what drives me.

People love to talk about the things I own, the success I've built, the public wins. But the thing I'm proudest of? It's not the closet, the cars, or the media attention. It's knowing that after every storm, every heartbreak, every setback, I chose to rise.

I've been bankrupt in spirit, even when my bank account was full. I've been lonely in a room packed with people. I've stared at myself in the mirror, questioning if I was enough, if I was worthy, if I could survive one more blow. And every single time, I chose to believe in my own comeback.

If you're reading this and wondering if **you** can rise, let me tell you right now: you absolutely can.

You already have everything you need inside you. That spark, that fight, that untouchable, unshakable part of you, it's there, even if you can't feel it right now.

I'm still building…Still dreaming…Still learning. I don't believe we ever truly "arrive." There's always another mountain to climb, another mission to pursue, another miracle waiting just around the corner.

Today, I am a proud member of **The Texas 100**, an entrepreneur, a coach, a philanthropist, a wife, a mother, a grandmother and a survivor.

I wake up each morning grateful, not because my life is perfect, but because it's beautiful *because* it's imperfect.

And if I can leave you with anything, let it be this:

Dream bigger than feels comfortable.
Work harder than feels fair.
Give more than feels safe.
Love deeper than feels reasonable.
And show up for your life like no one else will.

The life you want? It's not going to fall into your lap. You have to get up and build it, brick by brick, step by step, heartbreak by heartbreak.

I've stood on the mountain, arms raised in triumph, but I've also sat on the floor, shattered, wondering how I'd ever take another breath. And still, I rose.

The woman I am today is not the woman I was twenty years ago, or even five years ago. And thank God for that. Growth is painful. Reinvention is messy. But it's worth every scar, every bruise, every stretch.

I've learned that real strength isn't about never falling. It's about refusing to stay down. It's about looking life in the face and saying, **"You will not defeat me."**

So if you're facing a storm right now, if you're sitting in the ashes of something you thought would last forever, if you're questioning your worth, if you're wondering if you can survive this, hear me loud and clear:

You are stronger than you think.
You are braver than you feel.
You are more powerful than you know.
And you don't have to do it alone.

I will walk this journey with you. To remind you of your power. To challenge you. To lift you up when you can't lift yourself. To help you see that the woman (or man) you are becoming is already inside you, waiting.

I'm still just getting started.

And if you're ready, truly ready, I would be honored to help you build something extraordinary.

Together, let's rise. Let's dream. Let's fight. Let's love. Let's create a life so big, so bold, so beautiful, that you can look back and say, **"I lived every single moment fully."**

Because this one wild, precious life? It's yours to claim.

And I promise you: it's worth every single step.

EDWARD SANCHEZ

Edward Sanchez is one of Houston's most celebrated beauty professionals—an award-winning makeup artist, brow expert, and hair stylist whose artistry has earned recognition from **Vogue, Allure, Marie Claire, Vanity Fair,** and **Glamour**. Dubbed "*The Brow Whisperer*" by Vogue and named "*Best of the Best*" by *Allure* for three consecutive years, Sanchez is known for blending science, artistry, and precision in every transformation.

A graduate of the **University of Houston** with a degree in psychology, he also studied biochemistry at **Georgetown University**, nuclear medicine at the **National Institutes of Health**, and nursing at the **University of Texas–Pan American**. His diverse background informs a unique, holistic approach to beauty that merges aesthetics and wellness.

Sanchez began his career at **Foley's**, later managing luxury brands at **Neiman Marcus** and **Laura Mercier** before moving into the salon industry with **Trellis at The Houstonian, José Eber Salon,** and **Urban Retreat**. His clientele has included celebrities such as **Jennifer Aniston, Paula Abdul, George Clooney,** and **Queen Noor of Jordan**, as well as five U.S. presidents.

A dedicated philanthropist and three-time recipient of "**Edward Sanchez Day**" by the City of Houston, he serves on several arts boards and owns **ArchedBeauty Architects™**, home to his nationally recognized **BrowSmooth™** treatment.

ArchedBeauty.com   Instagram/Facebook/X/YouTube

CHAPTER 22

THE ARCHEDBEAUTY™ 4-D BROW REVOLUTION: REDEFINING THE FRAME OF THE FACE

By Edward Sanchez

Brows were always more than just hair to me; they were the frame to the soul. When I first discovered advanced threading and brow artistry in New York, I knew I had to bring something elevated back to Houston. What I saw in Manhattan was clinical, fast, and impersonal. What I envisioned was ritualistic, holistic, and artistic.

That is how I developed what I called ArchedBeauty™ 4-D Brows, a process that looked at the full dimension of the face, bone structure, age, and even skin elasticity. It was not just shaping it was architecture. I treated every brow like a blueprint, aligning angles, lifts, shadows, and hair patterns to create a customized look. I incorporated threading, waxing, tweezing, and tinting, not in isolation, but as elements of one precise execution.

When I introduced this to Houston, people were stunned; they had never seen brows treated with such reverence. Socialites were calling it "face-lifting without the surgery," and soon, brides, celebrities, and influencers started booking weeks out. That single innovation changed everything for me. It became a signature offering and a springboard for national recognition.

Keratin Brow and Lash Lamination

I studied Biology and Chemistry at the University of Texas and at the University of Houston. I needed a treatment to help tame and smooth unruly and wiry hairs without having to remove, trim, or cut them, so eyebrows grew in fuller and thicker. So, I developed a topical treatment that featured Keratin, revolutionizing the eyebrow game. Vogue and Allure Magazine touted this as a game-changer in the eyebrow business, and this catapulted me to Beverly Hills, where my business grew. Celebrities like Molly Ringwald, Jennifer Aniston, and Brooke Shields frequented the salon to receive eyebrow perfection.

Mentorship: Beauty Beyond the Brush

Of all the accolades and clients I've had the honor to work with, nothing has moved me more deeply than mentoring young talent. When I opened my first salon, I didn't want a traditional hierarchy; I wanted a creative lab. I've always believed that artistry grows best in shared light, not shadows.

Take Mariana, one of my earliest protégés. She was over 40, wore the thickest glasses I had ever seen, and had been turned away from two other salons for not having enough experience. I saw a spark. She had the softest hand with a brush and a natural instinct for color. I took her under my wing, gave her premium bridal clients, and let her shadow me for three months straight. Today, she's a six-figure artist with her own product line. Her success isn't just a feather in her cap; it's validation that investment in people is the ultimate ROI. There's also Chris, a barber-turned-brow artist, who approached me after watching one of my tutorials online. He had raw talent and a magnetic personality but no formal training. I invited him to the studio for a 10-day intensive. He stayed for a year, trained in ArchedBeauty™ 4-D Brow architecture, and now works full-time in The Galleria, commanding one of our most loyal male clientele.

I mentor not just for legacy, but because I was once mentored too. In the early days, before I was "Edward Sanchez," I had veterans who showed me how to blend tones, speak with elegance, and navigate clients with diplomacy. Mentorship is my way of honoring them and pushing the industry forward.

Celebrity Clients & Private Glamour

When collaborating with celebrities, it isn't about glitz, it's about trust. Stars are often the most vulnerable in the chair. They're exhausted, scrutinized, and in need of more than just a new face. They need peace of mind.

I'll never forget my first session with Molly Ringwald. Her energy was serene but strong. We talked about self-care, silence, and the importance of routine. She didn't want "Hollywood makeup," she wanted glow, grace, and softness. That session transformed how I approached high-profile clients. They didn't want masks, they wanted mirrors of their best selves, and accents of their most beautiful attributes, which could be their eyes, cheekbones, or even lips.

Joan Rivers, on the other hand, was everything you'd expect: sharp, hilarious, unfiltered. She wanted glam and didn't apologize for it. When working with Joan, she taught me the power of humor in the beauty chair and the grace in honoring a woman's right to feel fabulous at any age.

Queen Noor of Jordan was a magical experience. Even though there were so many rules of diplomacy that had to be respected for Her Majesty, not looking her directly in the eyes, always using Her Majesty when addressing her, and making sure no one could see me touching her. Even though the rules were very stringent, she was a down-to-earth, real-life person who wanted to feel and look beautiful from the inside and out, and our relationship lives on to this day.

I've worked on national campaigns, red carpet premieres, magazine covers, fashion shows, television shows, and movies, but the most meaningful moments are always human. A breast cancer survivor asking for brows to feel whole again. A grandmother, who thanked me for making her granddaughter bride feel like a queen after doing her hair and makeup, when I did the same for her and her daughter at their weddings. These are the encounters that anchor my entrepreneurial fire of purpose.

The Post Oak Chapter: Luxury, Reinvented

When I returned from California, I knew I didn't want to reenter the salon scene in the same way. I had grown. My clientele had grown. The expectations had changed. That's why I partnered with The Post Oak Hotel (Tillman Fertitta's five-star luxury property in the heart of Houston) and The Gold Nugget Casino in Lake Charles.

The idea was simple: elevate glam services to concierge-level hospitality. I created an in-house suite that felt like a sanctuary, plush, private, and meticulously designed. No walk-ins, no waiting, no rushed chairs. Every client receives champagne, a style consultation, and personalized artistry.

This wasn't just about aesthetics; it was about experience design. And it worked. Within the first 30 days, we were fully booked. Word spread among VIP circles, bridal planners, and even international guests. It felt like the culmination of everything I had learned: from my first brush stroke in retail to managing salons coast to coast. Post Oak became a metaphor for my brand: refined, grounded, and timeless.

Launching the Product Line: Beauty You Can Take Home

Clients often asked, "What did you use on me?" So, I began curating. I didn't want to white-label. I spent years developing formulas that respected skin diversity, Houston humidity, and long-wear durability.

My line began with brow powder and gel, followed by a hybrid highlighter and blush, and finally skin preps that hydrate without clogging. Every product is evaluated in my own salon on my real clients, in real time, with their feedback.

To me, launching a product line wasn't about scaling profit. It was about clients scaling access to artistry. Not everyone can sit in my chair, but they can experience the intention behind it. That's what the Edward Sanchez Cosmetics brand is all about: professional-grade quality made personal.

Failures, Detours, and What They Taught Me

Entrepreneurship is not a runway; it's a rocky hike. I've opened salons that failed. I invested in marketing that tanked. I have had business partners who just wanted my client list and stole my business. I once signed a lease in L.A. without thoroughly vetting zoning codes and had to delay my grand opening by six months; of course, COVID didn't help either. It was humiliating and expensive.

But I learned. I learned that contracts matter. That's because not all partnerships are aligned. A good team is not just talent, but rather its temperament, ethics, and communication. I've had employees and business partners steal clients. I've lost long-time regulars who moved or grew apart. I've experienced burnout and self-doubt, wondering if the industry still had room for someone like me. But every failure taught me to zoom out. To ask; What am I building? Who is it for? Why does it matter? These hard moments shaped my grit. They taught me to not just work in my business, but on it. Today, I delegate more, protect my boundaries, and lead with clarity. I'm not chasing trends. I'm cultivating a legacy.

Final Reflections: The Mirror I Hold Up to the World

I often say, "You can't create beauty if you don't recognize it in others." That's my ultimate mission, not just to shape brows or glam faces, but to help people see themselves. Whether it's the high-school girl prepping for prom or the billionaire stepping onto the red carpet, they're all searching for the same thing: to feel whole, powerful, and seen.

Leadership means guiding others toward their own radiance. Mentorship is lighting torches I didn't have. Entrepreneurship is believing that your vision, no matter how wild, can become structure, strategy, and story.

And so, I keep painting. I keep coaching. I keep dreaming.

Because beauty isn't just my business, it's my calling.

> **"Success, by many, is measured by how high you can reach, but I am amazed by how many paths it took to get there!"**
>
> -Edward Sanchez

"It is as if
a king had sent you to a country
to carry out one special, specific task.
You go to the country, and you perform a hundred other tasks,
but if you have not performed the task you were sent for,
it is as if you have done nothing at all".

–Rumi

TRACE J. SHERER

Trace J. Sherer is a storyteller, strategist, and survivor who believes in living life out loud. A retired trial attorney and seasoned mediator, Trace built a legal career marked by impact, first-chairing over 30 cases to verdict, handling complex appeals before the Texas Supreme Court, and teaching the next generation of lawyers as an adjunct professor at South Texas College of Law.

But it's not just the courtroom where Trace has shown resilience. Diagnosed with multiple sclerosis more than two decades ago, he's spent the years since refusing to be defined by a diagnosis. Instead, he's used it as fuel, to write, to speak, and to inspire others to live with courage, clarity, and conviction.

Trace is the author of Nerves of Steel, a raw and honest reflection on navigating life with MS, and Facelift, a sharp and compelling medical thriller. His unique voice, equal parts wit, wisdom, and grit, resonates with readers who crave both heart and intellect.

He lives in Houston with a dog who keeps him grounded and two diva cats who keep him humble. Whether he's mentoring young professionals, leading a mediation, or drafting his next book, Trace continues to advocate for a life lived fully, freely, and unapologetically out loud.

CHAPTER 23

DREAMING OUT LOUD

By Trace J. Sherer

That day in June 1999 started like any other June day in Houston, Texas. If you've ever been in Houston in the summer, you know what I mean -- it's like stepping into a sauna that forgot to turn off the humidity. The air was thick, sticky, and unforgiving. At the time, I was a trial lawyer focused on medical malpractice defense. Life was busy, and like most lawyers I knew, I pushed through pain, pressure, and anything that tried to slow me down.

But something wasn't right. I had a bit of back pain - nothing major - but then I started walking into walls. Literally. I figured I was overtired, maybe needed a steroid shot, and I'd be good to go. I happened to represent one of the biggest orthopedic groups in Houston, so I called one of my clients and told him I just needed a quick fix. He said, "Let's take a look first." I joked, "Hey, I'm not a doctor, but I play one in the courthouse." He laughed, then sent me across the street for a same-day visit with a neurologist, who immediately sent me for an MRI.

That day, I received a diagnosis that changed my life: Multiple Sclerosis. For many, it can take months, sometimes years, to get a diagnosis. I had mine in a matter of hours, but looking back, I realized my symptoms had been ignored by doctors... and me... for more than a decade. They were brushed off as stress, working too hard, drinking too much coffee. I rushed to get a second opinion, hoping maybe it was a mistake. That doctor told me I'd likely be in a wheelchair by the end of the year and might not make it past 2001. I took a breath. Then I did what I always do... I looked for options. I went back to the original neurologist - the one who didn't write me off - and told him I wanted to fight. I wanted to live, and live well. Thankfully, he was ready to walk that road with me.

For the next decade, I did pretty well. I cleaned up my diet, exercised regularly, and leaned into alternative approaches. One of my dearest friends, a holistic practitioner, had me try things that, at the time, sounded a little out there. She told me to have all my teeth with root canals removed because, according to her, they were blocking the flow of positive energy through my body. I said, "Why not?" The next day - swollen mouth and all - I played in a father-son soccer tournament. At one point, I was running across the field with one kid on my shoulders and another hanging on my feet. For a moment, I felt unstoppable. That might have been the only time anyone would've mistaken me for an athlete. And even that's a stretch.

But by 2010, the slow creep of MS started catching up with me. Things got harder. Walking, moving, doing everyday things that most people take for granted... I couldn't. And I noticed. One day, I had a case with a lawyer I'd never met before. Out of the blue, he showed up at my office. I greeted him in the hallway, barefoot, as I often was by then to ease the pain of pins and needles in my feet and toes. We ended up talking for three and a half hours about everything except the case. Before he left, he said, "I'm competing in the CB&I Triathlon this weekend. Why don't you come watch with my family?" He later told me that he suspected I was fighting something. He didn't know what exactly, but he saw it in me.

That encounter reminded me of something I had avoided for too long: vulnerability. I had built my career, my life, my image, on strength, control, and self-reliance. But MS has a way of stripping away whatever armor you think you have. It forces you to face parts of yourself you didn't want to admit were there, fear, pride, the quiet voice that wonders if you're becoming invisible. That lawyer saw me. Not just the trial lawyer, not just the guy with a limp, but the man inside who was holding on by sheer will. And it cracked something open in me. Maybe it was okay to let people see me. Maybe it was okay to stop pretending I had it all together.

That weekend, Houston heat was already creeping in, but I showed up anyway, hiding in the shade. When he crossed the finish line, he came straight to me and said, "Next year, you and I are doing this." I laughed. I couldn't walk across my office without getting winded, and this guy thought I could do a triathlon? The word "athlete" had never been in the same sentence as my name unless it was followed by the word "not." But he was serious. And maybe, deep down, I wanted to believe it was possible. He offered to meet me every Sunday to walk the run portion of the race. And for whatever reason - call it stubbornness, pride, hope - I said yes.

That was the beginning. And once I said yes, I took it seriously. I joined a gym. I hired a personal trainer. I started swimming, walking, lifting... whatever my body could handle that day, I did it. I didn't train like someone with MS. I trained like someone who wanted to compete. One day, after finishing a swim, a man approached me. "You have MS, don't you?" I said, "Yeah, I do." He handed me his t-shirt from that year's MS 150 bike ride and said, "Keep going. You're doing something great." At that moment, something shifted in me. I dreamed out loud... I told him I was going to do the triathlon. There. I said it. Out loud. He smiled and said he'd do it with me.

Word spread. My sons' classmates heard about it. Then their parents. Then teachers, nurses, doctors, engineers, lawyers - all kinds of people from all walks of life. People I had known for years and people I'd never met. They all said the same thing: "If you're doing it, we're doing it, too." The group wasl formed, and we had to name it. We called ourselves Team Inspiration Texas. We chose team colors. We trained. We supported each other. By race day, we had over 50 people on our team - walking, running, biking, cheering. All because one person was willing to say out loud what he hoped to do.

Looking back, I see how powerful that moment was, not just for me, but for everyone who joined the team. There's something transformative about saying your dream out loud, even when it feels impossible. Especially when it feels impossible. It creates a ripple you can't predict. And it creates a kind of sacred accountability. The minute I said I was going to do that triathlon, I wasn't just dreaming for myself anymore. I was dreaming for all the people who heard me say it. I was carrying their hope alongside mine. That's the gift, and the weight, of dreaming out loud. It stops being just your story. It becomes a community story. And that can push you through even the hardest training days.

The day of the race was brutal. The swim? Manageable. The bike ride? A battle. The run? I walked the whole thing. Kindergarteners were getting voting rights by the time I crossed the finish line with my sister, Kimi, and some of my best friends. The balloon arch was long gone. My mother and some other dear friends stood there, holding up the tattered remains of string flags as my finish line. It was perfect. Because here's the truth: it's not about how fast you get there. It's that you keep going. That you cross the line… your line… with integrity, courage, and a story to tell.

That was a long time ago now. And my body doesn't look or move the way it did then. MS has done what MS does - it's progressed. I'm in a wheelchair full-time these days. I can't walk the run portion anymore. I can't swim laps. I can't chase kids on the soccer field. But I can still choose how I show up. I can still choose my mindset. I can still dream out loud. I'd be lying if I said I don't miss those days. I miss the feeling of pushing my body, even when it pushed back. But more than anything, I miss the simplicity of it. The ability to just decide to move and move. Now, every movement is a process, a struggle, and most often, an impossibility. And yet, in some strange way, that's made the small, everyday things feel even more sacred. A great conversation. The sun on my face. Taking my dog for a walk alongside my wheelchair. I don't take those things for granted anymore. They feel like victories, too.

The truth is, this ethos - that we are not our diagnosis, that we are not our circumstances - it's not just something I said during my triathlon days. It's how I live now. Maybe more now than ever. Because the more your world shrinks physically, the more important it becomes to keep expanding it mentally, emotionally, spiritually. These days, dreaming out loud looks different for me. It's about showing up for my family. It's about being present in the lives of my kids, my sister, my nieces and nephews, my friends. It's about still finding the joy in small things - a good conversation, a story that makes me laugh, the simple, stubborn act of still being here on this earth, still trying, still loving this life.

And maybe most importantly, it's about reminding others - through my example - that even when your body quits cooperating, you can still lead. You can still choose your mindset. You can still light up a room. You can still be the person who says, "We're not done yet."

This journey... this fight... it's not just about MS. It's about life. It's about whatever battle you're facing. Maybe it's health. Maybe it's work. Maybe it's something nobody else even knows you're carrying. The point is, we all have something. And we all have a choice. You can let it define you, or you can decide who you are going to be in the middle of it. You can let the fear, the hard, the frustration own you. Or you can claim your space, your mindset, your story.

And you don't have to do it alone. Find your people. Even if it's just one or two. People who see you, not the thing you're fighting. People who won't flinch when you're having a hard day, but also won't let you camp there. Let them walk with you, sit with you, remind you of the parts of yourself that feel hard to see right now.

One of the biggest traps of any hard season, whether it's illness, loss, or failure, is isolation. It's easy to convince yourself that nobody gets it, that you're better off not burdening anyone with your mess. I've learned that's a lie MS loves to tell me. But the truth is, you don't need a stadium full of fans. You just need a handful of people who truly see you, who know the real you, and who will remind you of that when you forget. People who will sit with you in the hard times without trying to fix it, but who also won't let you stay stuck in it. Those people? They're gold. And they've saved me more than once. Control what you can control. Find the little wins. Name them. Celebrate them. Let them be enough. Because they are. You are. And when it feels overwhelming, when it feels like the darkness is bigger than you can handle, ask yourself: What's real right now? What can I do right now? And then do that thing.

Dream out loud. Not because it's easy. But because when you do, you invite others to dream alongside you. You create accountability, yes. But you also create a community. You create possibilities.

Because at the end of the day, it's not about finishing first. It's about finishing fully alive, fully you, and maybe, just maybe, helping someone else believe they can do the same.

That's what dreaming out loud is all about.

And it still is.

There is a thinking stuff from which all things are made, and which, in its original state, permeates, penetrates, and fills the interspaces of the universe. A thought in this substance produces the thing that is imagined by the thought.
A person can form things in his thought, and, by impressing his thought upon formless substance, can cause the thing he thinks about to be created.

—Wallace Wattles

SABA SYED

Saba Syed is the founder and owner of **Oasis Moroccan Bath**, Houston's premier luxury spa dedicated to authentic hammam rituals and modern beauty experiences. Blending centuries-old Moroccan traditions with contemporary comfort, she has created a sanctuary of serenity where every guest feels seen, valued, and restored. Her vision combines artistry, hospitality, and cultural heritage to deliver a spa experience that transcends self-care—offering renewal for both body and soul.

By introducing the Houston market to French and Moroccan organic beauty products, steam therapy, and time-honored exfoliation and nourishment treatments, Syed has established Oasis Moroccan Bath as a leader in luxury wellness. Her spa has been featured in local media and has welcomed celebrities and professional athletes from **the Houston Texans, Rockets,** and **Dynamo**, drawn by its transformative treatments and personalized service.

Beyond entrepreneurship, Syed is a devoted single mother of four, an author, and an advocate for women's empowerment. Her award-winning book, *An Acquaintance*, reflects her mission to uplift others through resilience and truth. A proud Houstonian with Pakistani heritage, she continues to inspire through her philanthropy, public speaking, and unwavering belief that healing—whether physical, emotional, or spiritual—begins with self-love and courage.

OasisMoroccanBath.com   Instagram.com/oasismoroccanbath

CHAPTER 24

RISING FROM WITHIN

By Saba Syed

When people walk into Oasis Moroccan Bath, they often comment on the calm that greets them, the soft scents of eucalyptus and orange blossom, and the warm welcome that quiets the noise of the outside world. What they may not see, however, is the story behind this sanctuary, a journey of faith, struggle, resilience, and the quiet power of starting over.

A Dream Rooted in Faith and Persistence

I am Saba Syed, the founder and owner of Oasis Moroccan Bath. I did not initially set out to become a business owner. I was a stay-at-home mother of four and had spent 25 years in a marriage before deciding to leave and rebuild my life. For me, leaving my marriage was not merely a turning point; it was also a promise to my children to create a safe and beautiful future.

The journey was anything but easy. I found myself standing at the edge of the unknown, facing a world that often underestimated me, especially as a Muslim woman of color. I had no roadmap for navigating single motherhood while building a new business, nor did I have a clear blueprint for entrepreneurship. Yet, what I did have was an unshakable faith in God's guidance, a commitment to hard work, and a lifelong passion for nurturing others.

Choosing a Unique Business Idea

The idea of opening a luxury Hammam spa in Houston was, in many ways, radical. Hammam rituals, while very popular in North Africa, the Middle East, and even Europe, were virtually unknown in the American wellness market. Most people associate spas with massages and facials, but the concept of steam therapy, using high-quality products, vigorous exfoliation, and full-body oil treatments, feels foreign to many. During my travels overseas, I witnessed firsthand how these rituals could transform the skin while restoring a deep sense of inner calm. I knew my hometown of Houston needed a place like this, a space where people could detoxify, unwind, and experience centuries-old traditions in a luxurious and welcoming setting.

I also realized that bringing these traditions to Houston would be an uphill battle, requiring me to educate a market unfamiliar with hammam rituals and convince clients to trust the benefits of these treatments and my vision. It would mean overcoming the hesitation that often comes when something feels different or foreign. It would require building trust through consistency, hospitality, and genuine care.

However, I wasn't just introducing a new concept; I was determined to maintain a high standard of quality from the outset. Every element mattered: constructing a serene space, importing authentic decor, hand-picking luxury organic products from Africa and Europe, and selecting staff I could trust to care for clients with the same dedication I held in my heart. This required more than dedication; it required conviction that each decision would build a brand defined by exclusivity and luxury.

The Challenges of Being a First-Time Business Owner

Establishing Oasis Moroccan Bath was a path lined with challenges that demanded every ounce of my faith and perseverance. As a first-time business owner, I faced a steep learning curve in every area, from sourcing authentic, high-quality products while managing costs to designing a space that felt like a "sanctuary of tranquility" within city limits. Building a brand from scratch meant designing the spa, handling permits and inspections, hiring and training staff, and creating a marketing plan, all while ensuring my children's needs were met at home.

Marketing required creativity and resilience, especially when initial advertisements yielded little response. There were moments of doubt, times when fear whispered that it would be easier to give up and take a safer path. But I could not give up. The business was more than just a spa; it was my way of leaving a legacy for my children, a symbol of my courage, and a demonstration that faith, hard work, and trust in God can transform even the most daunting dreams into reality.

The Motivation to Leave a Legacy

I wanted my children to see me build something meaningful, to understand that while the world may place limitations on what women and minorities can achieve, faith, dedication, and resilience can break through those barriers. Each success was a quiet message to my children that they, too, could build their dreams, no matter how intimidating the path might seem.

For me, Oasis Moroccan Bath was never just about offering wellness services; it was about creating a sanctuary for women, particularly those who carried heavy emotional and physical burdens, to experience a space where they felt seen, valued, and renewed. Each guest who walked through the doors became a reminder of why I embarked on this path. Every grateful smile, every sigh of relief from a guest leaving a treatment, every story shared in the quiet spaces of the spa was a testament that this was bigger than me or a business. It was a mission, a calling, and a legacy I was building not only for myself, but especially for my children and my community.

The Power of Women Supporting Women

As a Muslim woman of color navigating business ownership, there were moments when I felt isolated. It is not easy to balance cultural expectations with entrepreneurial aspirations, nor is it easy to face the added scrutiny that often accompanies underrepresented women entering industries dominated by others. Yet, in those moments of fear and uncertainty, I found strength in the quiet, powerful bonds I formed with other women. There were moments when a simple, kind word from another woman, a whispered prayer, or a shared story of perseverance provided the comfort and encouragement I needed to keep going.

This bond of empowerment among women became a unique aspect of my journey, reminding me that when women uplift each other, we create ripples of impact far beyond our individual goals, strengthening families and communities in profound ways.

Milestones and Growth

Despite the challenges, Oasis Moroccan Bath continued to grow steadily. Within the first two years, it was featured on local television and in prominent Houston magazines, highlighting its unique treatments and the exceptional hospitality that set it apart. Initially hesitant to try hammam rituals, clients became loyal guests. Celebrities, professional athletes from the Houston Texans, Rockets, and Dynamo, as well as community leaders, began to visit the spa, further solidifying its reputation. I still remember when I first opened the spa, quietly dreaming of one day being featured on television. It felt distant and unrealistic at the time. But just months after our first anniversary,

CW39 reached out for an interview. Tears welled up in my eyes as I realized that dreams do come true if you keep faith and keep trying.

In under three years, Oasis Moroccan Bath became a recognized luxury wellness brand, and the demand for its services led to plans for expansion into other cities. What began as a small, uncertain dream had blossomed into a thriving business, touching the lives of many while preserving the authenticity of hammam traditions in a luxury setting.

Lessons Learned Along the Way

My journey as a first-time business owner navigating personal and professional transitions has definitely taught me invaluable lessons:

- **Education is essential:** Introducing a new concept requires time, patience, and a willingness to educate the audience. Many people mistook my spa for a "public bathing house," and I had to devise innovative marketing approaches to demonstrate to the community that our spa offered private, luxurious experiences rooted in rich traditions.
- **Faith fuels resilience:** In moments of doubt, my faith anchored me. I learned to lean into prayer, to trust in God's timing, and to view challenges as opportunities for growth rather than setbacks. When I reached out to luxury hotels for collaborations early on, I faced rejection, which was disheartening. Yet, I trusted the process, and less than two years later, those same hotels reached out to collaborate.
- **Community matters:** The support of other women and the loyalty of clients became the foundation of the spa's growth. Building genuine relationships and treating clients as family fostered trust that fueled organic growth.
- **You don't have to know everything to begin:** Starting a business can be intimidating, especially when you are stepping

into a new industry. Taking one step at a time and remaining open to learning makes the journey possible and successful.

- **Self-care is essential for leaders, too. As someone driven by purpose, I learned that prioritizing self-care was not a luxury, but a necessity for my well-being and the sustainability of my** business and my role as a mother. My spa became a reminder to me, to pause, breathe, and restore.

Advice for Aspiring Entrepreneurs

If I could offer guidance to others considering entrepreneurship, especially women and minorities, I would say this:

- **Trust your vision:** Your idea may seem radical to others, but it's yours for a reason. Research it well, understand your challenges, and once you commit, hold onto your vision with persistence.
- **Start where you are:** Perfection is not required to begin. My first location wasn't the ideal size I envisioned, but it had the right rent and location, so I moved forward and made it the tranquil oasis I envisioned for my guests.
- **Be selective with advice.** Seek guidance, but be discerning about who you listen to. Not everyone will understand your journey or your vision, and many will project their failures and fears onto you. Tune out unnecessary noise and trust voices with relevant experience.
- **Honor your values:** Let your faith and your vision guide your decisions. These are strengths that add depth and authenticity to your business.
- **Remember your 'why':** When challenges arise, return to the reason you started. Let your purpose fuel you on difficult days. And remember, with difficulty comes ease.

- **Stress is part of the process.** It's okay to feel stressed, but learn to manage it. In fact, I believe if you're not waking up in the middle of the night thinking about how to grow your business or solve its challenges, you're not fully invested in its success.

A Legacy for the Future

To me, the success of Oasis Moroccan Bath is not defined solely by profit margins, but by the lives touched, the women empowered, and the example set for my children. My children have witnessed the hard work, the challenges, and the moments of doubt transformed into perseverance. They have seen me live my values, care for my staff and clients with dignity, and stand firmly in my identity while creating a business rooted in excellence.

Oasis Moroccan Bath is more than a spa; it is a testament to what is possible when a woman chooses to rise, even when the odds are stacked against her. It demonstrates the power of faith, the beauty of old rituals and traditions, and the quiet, steady strength of a mother determined to leave a legacy of strength and hope.

Closing Reflection

As guests leave Oasis Moroccan Bath, carrying with them the calm and renewal they experienced, they carry a piece of my vision and story with them. It is a reminder that every act of care, every step toward healing, and every moment of rest is an act of courage in a world that often demands constant giving. Through my work, I continue to champion the cause of women's empowerment, using my business as a platform to uplift others while staying true to myself. My story is not just about building a business; it is about building hope and proving that even when starting over, one can create something lasting, meaningful, and beautiful. For anyone standing at the edge of change, I hope my journey serves as a gentle reminder: you can rise and build something that matters. Just remember, one step, one prayer, and one act of courage at a time.

PETER C. REMINGTON

Peter Remington is the founder and Chief Possibility Officer of **Prepare 4 More**, a self-development company dedicated to helping individuals and organizations achieve their fullest potential through purpose-driven strategies and actionable coaching. A dynamic speaker, author, and entrepreneur, he has trained more than three thousand professionals, empowering them to clarify their vision, define their purpose, and build lasting success.

Peter is also the co-founder of **Remington Insurance Brokers**, launched with his wife and business partner, Karen De Geurin, the company's president. Together, they provide personalized insurance solutions with a client-first approach, specializing in Medicare, Medicaid, and group and individual policies.

The best-selling author of *Be-Aholic: A 14-Step Process to Becoming a Success-Aholic*, Peter has led trainings for organizations such as **Lakewood Church**, the **Houston Astros**, the **American Cancer Society**, and **J.W. Marriott**. Holding an **M.B.A. from the University of Georgia**, he is a triple-certified Life Mastery Consultant and the founder of **Cheers 4 Charities**, a nonprofit supporting children's causes.

Peter also serves on the **Board of Directors for Kids' Meals** and the **Houston Livestock Show and Rodeo Speaker Committee**. In his free time, he enjoys reading, writing, skiing, traveling, and participating in Spain's Running of the Bulls. A man of faith, grit, and loyalty, Peter believes in hard work, humanity, and standing up for what's right. He and Karen live happily with their two beloved dogs.

> "The temptation to quit is always the strongest just before you succeed."

PeterRemington.com/insights

CHAPTER 25

HOW TO BECOME A SWINGER!

By Peter C. Remington

While listening to the radio, the song "It doesn't mean a thing if it ain't got that swing" came on, being sung by Tony Bennet and Lady Gaga. Then I thought, if you just change one word in the title of this song, you'll have a mantra for Life…. YOU don't mean a thing if you ain't got that S.W.I.N.G.! Today, I am going to write about how to become a S.W.I.N.G.E.R!

Having been around, trained, coached, and mentored thousands of salespeople, managers, and general managers in various careers over my 40-plus-year career, I have noticed that 2% of the salespeople make 90% of the money. Like 2% of the population makes 90% of the money in America. I have heard too many times that someone's career isn't brain surgery. But then again…they're not brain surgeons. But they should act like one in their career. In other words,…Brain Surgeons know how to be S.W.I.N.G.E.R.s… and so should you. You should become a S.W.I.N.G.E.R. or you will be working for someone who is. To become a S.W.I.N.G.E.R you need to have:

Specialized Knowledge

Specialized knowledge means increasing your skill set beyond the basics, becoming a lifelong student of your craft. Too many individuals stop their education the moment they walk across the graduation stage, assuming the diploma is the end of learning. In reality, it should be the beginning. Statistics show that the majority of college graduates don't read a single book a year after graduation. That is a staggering fact, one that separates the average from the exceptional. In today's hyper-competitive marketplace, information is currency, and skill is leverage. If you want to stand out in your organization, you must continuously invest in your development. Study your industry, stay updated with trends, master the tools that others neglect, and pursue certifications or trainings that elevate your competency. Ask questions no one else is asking. Seek mentors who have achieved what you desire. Learn not just the "what" but the "why" behind your business. When you cultivate knowledge others overlook, you become indispensable. You are not just another employee, you are a resource, a strategist, a problem-solver. That's what specialized knowledge does: it empowers you to lead, innovate, and shape the future instead of reacting to it. Growth isn't optional; it's strategic.

Why are you doing what you are doing?

Understanding the "why" behind what you do is the foundation of a fulfilling and impactful life. Without a clear purpose, even the most exciting job can become a burden, and success can feel empty. Your "why" gives meaning to your actions, energizes your ambitions, and serves as the compass that guides you through challenges and triumphs. It's the emotional heartbeat of your career, your family life, your dreams. Without it, you may achieve external success but feel internal disconnection. Discovering your "why" requires introspection, asking yourself hard questions about what truly drives you. Is it to make a difference in the lives of others? Is it to break generational cycles? Is it to express your unique gifts in a way only you can? When your "why" is clear, everything aligns: your decisions, your discipline, your resilience. It is the gravitational center of the S.W.I.N.G.E.R. philosophy. Everything, the specialized knowledge, integrity, nurturing, grit, execution, and rituals, revolves around your why. It's not about what you do but why you do it. Find your purpose, and you'll find your power. Anchor yourself to it, and no setback will ever fully shake you. Your "why" is your reason to rise.

Integrity

Integrity is more than just doing the right thing when no one is watching, it is the alignment of your thoughts, words, and actions. It starts with your thoughts, because what you think, you eventually speak. What you speak, you begin to act upon. Over time, your actions become habits, your habits define your values, and your values shape your destiny. Integrity is not about perfection, but consistency. It is the internal compass that helps you choose the high road, even when it's the harder path. When your words match your actions, you earn trust. When your behavior is consistent with your values, you build credibility. Integrity isn't something you put on like a jacket for business meetings or public appearances, it's who you are when it's inconvenient, when no one else is around, when the stakes are high. Living with integrity simplifies life, because you no longer have to remember what version of yourself you showed to different people. You are whole. You are authentic. And because of that, your influence expands. People gravitate toward leaders of character. The S.W.I.N.G.E.R. is grounded in integrity because without it, everything else collapses. It is the root of true success.

Nurture those around you

What good is a life if it doesn't light the path for someone else? Nurturing is about passing on wisdom, offering encouragement, sharing time, and helping others grow into their own greatness. It's a commitment to multiplying impact, not just achieving for yourself, but helping others rise with you. Whether you're mentoring a young professional, raising a child, or simply offering a listening ear to a colleague, nurturing is an act of service that extends your legacy. True leaders don't hoard knowledge or guard their success like a secret, they create opportunities for others to flourish. In the S.W.I.N.G.E.R. philosophy, nurturing means being generous with your journey. It's about pulling someone else up the ladder, knowing that the climb is easier when someone shows you the footholds. And remember, nurturing isn't about perfection, it's about presence. It's about seeing potential in someone even when they don't see it in themselves and helping them cultivate it until they do. The world needs more encouragers, more builders, more givers. Be that person. The ripple effect of nurturing can't be measured, but it is always felt. Your greatest contribution might not be something you do, it might be someone you helped become who they are.

Grit

Grit is the quiet force behind every remarkable achievement. It's not flashy or glamorous, but it's relentless. It's waking up early when you're tired, making the calls when you're discouraged, showing up again and again when others have quit. Grit means staying the course even when you don't see immediate results. It's the decision to push forward when the finish line feels a mile away. Talent may open the door, but grit walks you through it. Intelligence can get you started, but tenacity finishes the job. Grit is the fuel that powers execution, learning, and reinvention. It is built in the small moments, when you choose effort over excuses, commitment over comfort. It is strengthened every time you do what you said you'd do, even when the initial excitement has faded. Swingers who possess grit are leaders others can count on. They bring reliability, consistency, and perseverance to every project. They understand that success isn't about having it easy; it's about enduring the hard. You don't need to be the most talented or the most connected, you just need to be the one who refuses to give up. Grit separates dabblers from doers, dreamers from achievers.

Execution

Vision without execution is hallucination. Ideas are cheap, everyone has them. But turning an idea into a tangible outcome requires discipline, focus, and daily follow-through. Execution is where greatness is built. It's in the daily grind, the often unseen and uncelebrated actions that move you closer to your goal. Swingers understand that success is earned in inches, not miles. They don't wait for the perfect moment, they create momentum through consistent effort. That means making the call, completing the report, holding the meeting, or reviewing the numbers, every single day. It means finishing your day with your plate clean, knowing that nothing was left for others to pick up. Execution is about being dependable and proactive. It's not about speed; it's about completeness and excellence. Plans without execution are just dreams. Swingers don't just plan, they perform. They don't just start, they finish. If you want to stand out, be the person who delivers, not just once, but every time. Consistency compounds. One small win each day creates big wins over time. That's the S.W.I.N.G.E.R. way, finish what you start, do what you promise, and let your work ethic speak louder than your words.

Rituals

Rituals are the anchors that keep you grounded and aligned. They are intentional, repeated actions that create rhythm, discipline, and balance in your life. Rituals are not routines done out of obligation, they are purposeful habits designed to elevate your performance and deepen your peace. For Swingers, rituals may include morning meditation, journaling, exercise, spiritual reflection, reading, or strategic planning. These acts keep the mind clear, the body strong, and the spirit centered.

Without rituals, life can easily become chaotic, and chaos is the enemy of clarity. Rituals help you show up as your best self, regardless of the external noise. They create structure in the midst of unpredictability. When practiced consistently, rituals shape your identity. They reinforce your values and help you return to your purpose when distractions arise. They're how you tune out the world and tune into yourself. In a culture obsessed with hustle, rituals remind you to pause, reflect, and recalibrate. They create space for creativity, gratitude, and intentionality. If you want to sustain long-term excellence, not just short bursts of performance, develop rituals that feed your mind, body, and soul. Rituals aren't luxuries; they're necessities for those aiming to lead and last.

Open your heart and mind to the part of you that is bigger than the part you have been playing. Search the areas of your life and identify where you need to improve, then put a plan into action.

You will soon find out that;

"You do mean a thing, because you got that SWING."

Become a S.W.I.N.G.E.R!

Some Words to Thrive by

–Peter C. Remington

Yesterday's knowledge doesn't solve today's problems.

It's better to be prepared without an opportunity than to have an opportunity and not be prepared.

The pain endured while making a vision happen doesn't last nearly as long, as the pain endured knowing you quit.

Lack of evidence is not evidence of lack. Keep the faith and never give up.

You cannot gain an hour of time by worrying, 98% of the things you worry about don't happen.

Obstacles are only obstacle-illusions.

You don't have to be great to get started…you do have to get started to become great.

Life without ACTION is a painting. ACTION is the thing that gets you off the canvas and on to the playing field.

You cannot conquer what you don't confront.

YOU WILL GROW AS HIGH AS YOUR-BELIEF IN YOURSELF.

Your name is your currency.

Live life as if it is stacked in your favor…

www.ingramcontent.com/pod-product-compliance
Lightning Source LLC
LaVergne TN
LVHW021331080526
838202LV00003B/141